From Where I Sit

by Stephen Brown

Copyright © 2019 Stephen Brown

All rights reserved.

ISBN 9781078150088

INTRODUCTION

About the author – of brother, neighbor, husband, daddy, and any other role God and man may have cast upon me, I try to weather each to the very best of my ability. I love Jesus, frosty mornings and fried okra.

Anything else about me is really insignificant.

As a family, we are tucked back in the woods seven or eight miles from our one-red-light town. Life for us is very basic, rustic by most standards. The short stories that follow are comprised of actual events of any given day in our lives.

We hunt and fish to fill the freezer, we pray and grow much of what we eat, and bathe outside. We laugh and love, scream and cry, bleed and die like everyone else.

The written prose here is identical to our spoken dialect. Lower Wewahitchkan, as I call it. A southern drawl with a touch of hillbilly, or so I'm told. These stories are written politically incorrect and without much apology.

We live with and love our pets and respect our veterans. We willingly share our faith, our broken hearts, and hopes and dreams of a better tomorrow with equal fervor.

There are four of us under our humble roof, but we do our best to exist as one.

It is my simple desire that you enjoy, laugh and somehow relate to the following stories of our day to day lives.

Table of Contents

1.	Workin for Peanuts	7
2.	School's Out	12
3.	The River Camp	18
4.	Blind Date	24
5.	So Long, Ol' Friend	29
6.	The Bricks	31
7.	Lightnin Bugs	35
8.	Long Beards 'n Leotards	38
9.	The Whole World on a Shelf	42
10.	From Where I Sit	45
11.	Moses	49
12.	Chicken Talk	53
13.	The Barn	57
14.	A Good Neighbor	61
15.	Facing My Demons	66
16.	Bea Bea Bugs	69
17.	Mother's Day 'n May Flies	73
18.	A Day with Beau	77
19.	Our Most Precious Commodity	82
20.	Piddlin	86

21. Cuteness 'n Carnage	90
22. Will It Really Matter in a Hunerd Years?	94
23. Watching Each Other	98
24. Empty Chairs	102
25. Twas Early September	105
26. Sandal Prints	109
27. 10th of October 2018	113
28. A Daughter's Request	118
29. The Spot	122
30. Finally	126
31. Two Bears	128
32. Daydreaming	132
33. Eyes Wide Open	137
34. Growin Up 'n Catchin On	140
35. Take Nothing for Granted	144
36. Heroes Walk Among Us	148
37. Mariah's Buck	152
38. The Circle of Rabbits	157
39. We Blendeth Not	161
40. Pass the Grits	167
Acknowledgements	171

Workin for Peanuts

Quite chilly was the morning when Mama shook me from a peaceful slumber. I was toasty warm from the neck down but could see frost on my breath as I peeked from under a pile of hand sewn blankets. I remember trying to blow a circle like an Indian sending a smoke signal on a Saturday morning western. There were immediate chores to do, take out the trash and feed the dog, but the first one was to scan the floor for a pair of warm, matching socks. I really didn't care whether they matched or not.

The pleasant blend of roasting peanuts and bacon wafting through the house helped stir a young lad into motion. I was five years old and this ritual happened every Saturday morning rain or shine, beginning in mid-September and continued until the peanuts ran out.

Mama's brother was a peanut farmer in Jackson County and each year she and Daddy'd buy forty pounds or so to be peddled on our hometown sidewalks. This was my parents' way of introducing a young lad to basic economics. It also served as a deterrent to their theory of 'idle hands' for an imaginative little boy.

Once the peanuts came outa the oven, thirty brown paper bags were filled and placed into a 'Walker boot box' from Daddy's shoe store. Daddy had tied a thin leather strap to the box so I could wear it around my neck. Some days, like the peanuts, were better than others, but the instructions were clear, don't come back till they're all sold. *And off I'd go…*

Sometimes Mr. Poley, our next-door neighbor, would be singing on his front porch and he would be my first sale. Next stop was Dr. Canning's doctor's office on the corner where Ms. Nellie would be tending to folks. It was always quiet in there and I liked it. I'd then cross the street and climb the steps into Lister's hardware.

Unbeknownst at the time, this was my first introduction to a two-story 'Man Mall.' I was forevermore intrigued by this old store and always lingered there.

Up and down the sidewalks of our quaint town I walked - *with a boot box around my neck.* "Peanuts 10¢" scribbled across the front. I'd walk to the Jr. Food where Ms. Martha would always buy a bag, then amble past the Mojo station and the Suwanee store where old men sat and spat on the wooden bench outside. On to the bank, Mrs. Lorrain Norton's flower shop, Lanier's Variety to see Ms. Dee. Then to Black's dry cleaners where Mrs. Davis would always stop those big steam presses and indulge a young boy with twenty cents. Rounding the corner to Gaskin-Graddy Insurance on back street was usually my next stop.

This is where I'd come full circle and was back close to home. Most times I'd sold out by now, sometimes not. If there were a few bags left, I'd head straight to the barber shop where many a pair of overalls sat waiting their turn. And inside those overalls were dimes. I liked to end up here so I could hang out a bit...... *and listen.*

On occasion I had to approach a total stranger and ask if they'd like to buy a bag. Being the shy lad I was at five whole years, I didn't cotton much for conversation. Maybe that's why my folks insisted on this endeavor.

I didn't even know how to make change, if someone handed me a case-quarter for a 10¢ bag, I'd simply hold out my hand so they could make their own change. I remember this bothered me some, it was as if I was not totally self-sufficient in my task.

With an empty box and a heavy jingle in my pocket I returned home. I'd empty my pockets on the faded linoleum table in the kitchen and the real lesson began. Mama'd stack up the coins, three stacks, one dollar each. In her apron pocket she'd put one stack of dimes to cover the cost of the peanuts. Then she'd take another stack she'd say, to cover the cost of the bags and her labor of cooking them. The last stack was mine, minus ten cents for tithe in Sunday school tomorrow and twenty cents into the piggy bank on the shelf.

For the briefest of moments, with seventy cents in my pocket and grape flavored bubble gum within walking distance............ *I knew how it felt to be a Rockefeller.*

Photo courtesy of Scotty Brown

School's Out

There was no need for my brother and I to be reminded to brush our teeth on this day, or comb our hair, tuck in our shirts or to wear a belt. On this day we were at the table on time dressed and ready as we should be. Some of these actions I took offense to, not because of a rebellious nature (*that came later*) but because my inner being simply screamed for loose clothing and bare feet.

Daddy made breakfast most weekday mornings as Mama usually was at work early for bus or lunchroom duty or some other task that schoolteachers had to contend with. A daddy-breakfast was typically a plate of biscuits from a box of Bisquick and bacon or patty sausage; Daddy always had meat.

Wanting to end the year on a magical note I ran to the corner of Second Street and River Road and waited for the familiar 'clippity-clop clippity-clop' that signified my ride was approaching. A simple thing really, but to a seven-year-old it was monumental. Cottle Johnson drove his one-mule slop wagon most days to the school to pick up the refuse and sometimes he'd let me tag along. "Get'm up, Ped" and off we'd go as I climbed aboard. Arriving at school barefoot on a bicycle with a banana seat was one thing but being the sole passenger on a rocket ship slop wagon was another. Celebrity status was hence bestowed on a second grader.

When the last bell rang and school was out for the summer, another life began for a Wewa youngster. Mind you, there were plenty of chores to do if you continued to eat and sleep in Mama's house. There was grass to cut, leaves to rake and wood to split for the fall. Daddy used to say, "I hope this wood keeps me as warm in December as it does now in June."

Once I was tall enough to see over the lawn mower handle, I graduated from selling peanuts to doing odd jobs around the neighborhood and in the shoe shop. Mostly without pay. Mama referred to this as, 'civic duty.' I didn't know what the heck 'civic duty' meant, but I did know I was expected to walk to the Post Office and get the mail for Ms. Rhetta Rish, our neighbor on the east side. She was a quaint, very kind lady, about a hundred and forty or fifty years old. She always kept a jar of M&M's front and center on the coffee table in her immaculate living room. And a young boy had a permanent hankering for chocolate.

Maw Dee, Mr. Poley's wife, was bed-ridden and our neighbor on the other side. Per Mama, I'd make the mail run for them also, I didn't mind because sometimes, though I was too small to crack it, Mr. Poley'd let me hold his leather bull whip that hung on a nail on his back porch. This he used to keep his chickens from wandering off. I would almost always hear a fascinating story about a paddle-wheel boat. Other times he'd be working on building replicas of those boats in his shed across the alley and would indulge a little boy by 'letting him help.'

All of this would happen AFTER.

After me n Billy Mc met at McGlon's service station on the corner before the town woke up good. On our second-hand bicycles we'd take off in different directions. Gathering coke bottles was our mission, and we needed at least fifteen or maybe sixteen for good measure. We would cash them in at the Jr. Food store for a nickel a piece. This was about seventy-five or eighty cents worth, and we didn't have to use all our fingers and toes to figure it out.

This was enough to guarantee each of us a Coca-Cola and a candy bar. Most critically of all, it left enough to pay Mr. Lightfoot for a can of store-bought wigglers. Mr. Lightfoot lived on the north side of Lake Alice behind Gil and Lynda Gayle Shealy. Under a big oak tree he had an impressive wiggler bed in his front yard. He'd sell us twenty-four wigglers for twenty-five cents, "and a penny tax" he'd say.

Why we went to this trouble, I can't rightly recall. Wigglers were easy enough to dig up and much quicker than the process we put ourselves through. Maybe it was the conversation with Mr. Lightfoot, perhaps it was scouring the streets on our bikes or possibly it was trimming the bamboo with our Barlow pocketknives. Looking back, I just don't know.

Billy Mc was good at picking out just the right cane pole, not too stiff, not too green, not too limber. There was a good stand of bamboo behind Wewa Bank next to the lake. We'd cut down a couple and string'em with line and cork from either his daddy's tackle box or mine. And for these efforts, many a bass, bream and polliwog were flung onto the bank from Lake Alice.

Round and round the lake we'd circle watching the cork with a store-bought worm on the end of the line. On the hottest days we'd come home soaking wet. "No Mama, we weren't swimming.

We just had to wade out and unhook from a tangle. And it was deep!"

There has been ample mud squeezed between the toes of me and Billy Mc and many others around those lakes. I'm not sure what a seven-year-old does now-a-days after the last bell has rung, but grateful am I for the memories of bamboo, store bought wigglers and five cent coke bottles. But most of all, for the sense of freedom that came with them.

The River Camp

It was the summer of my fourteenth year, the fifteenth for J. Frank and there would be very few idle hours for us. We had been duly prepped for what was coming, for the sweat was about to begin.

There had been a house fire in town next to the community building and fortunately no one was hurt. For most passersby the charred ruins of this ol' shotgun house now appeared little more than smoldering rubble harboring a lifetime of precious memories. Frank Graddy saw something else.

A few days later it was announced to J. Frank and I that an agreement had been reached for the structure to be torn down and the lot cleaned off in exchange for the remaining lumber. Seemed like a win – win for both parties, except J. Frank and me.

School was out, the air was warm, and the creek was cold, there were fish to catch and skirts to chase. For a fourteen-year-old boy much time and strategy were involved in matters of the latter. And for two teenagers, house demolition was nowhere close to the top of our priority list. While our friends were frolicking away the endless, long peaceful days of summer, we arose early and sweated.

Mr. Frank had a dream and the boards came down, six-inch fat lighter'd tongue-n-groove boards on the walls, two-inch in the flooring. The original carpenter was exceptional at his trade craft and had intended on this house standing firm right through the battle of Armageddon. Salvaging this lumber was a slow, tedious and laborious task.

To speed things up Mr. Frank devised a coupla tools and fashioned them with bent flat iron and long handles for leverage that unhinged the boards easily from their reluctant position....... ingenious actually.

On rickety sawhorses we cut and stacked piles of lumber between their house and Preacher Glass. We backed out hundreds of nails then bent them straight again. Little was wasted for there was a camp to build. The hot days of summer passed and so did the girls on their way to the lake. We sweated.

A month later and down to the last few boards, we heard the fire whistle go off again and both knew what that meant.

Two of our teenage summers was the cost for enough material to be salvaged before the real work began. And it began on a Saturday morning boat ride up Big River to select a location. Mr. Frank quickly decided on a spot on the Liberty County side at mile marker forty-eight. Under his direction, chainsaws and axes soon turned a dense river ridge into a promise in a day's time.

It rained that day, all day, which was fine with me except that it helped spread the poison ivy into undesirable places.

Long, heavy light poles were later trailered into Porter's Lake then floated down stream and finally hauled ashore. Acquaintance with a set of post hole diggers is still fresh to memory now forty years later. One boat load at the time the mass accumulation of boards was barged upriver and soon Mr. Frank's dream began to take shape. I'll admit at the time I hadn't yet begun to envision his fancy because rolling sweat, and poison ivy brought little satisfaction to a now fifteen-year-old lad.

The hottest day recorded in a thousand years was on a Saturday in July 1977, Kinard Creek was at it's clearest and a huge party was planned on her banks. Every scantily clad girl in nine counties was going to be there. Mr. Frank decided this would be the perfect day to hoist and lay the huge floor joists for a thirty by thirty room six feet off the ground with a ten by thirty-foot front porch. My back ached and my mind was numb. During a well-deserved six-minute break I stood in the shade overlooking Big River. The shimmer and ripple of the slow flowing waters was mesmerizing to an adolescent mind. I heard nothing but the rustle of leaves on a breeze. These elements of nature spoke to me that day and I absorbed it. Long before the walls came up, I began to envision what he already knew.

After that moment the work didn't seem as laborious. As my drill Sergeant used to say, "Get your mind right and the body will follow."

The last nail was finally driven in late summer of 1978. It was one of two defining moments for me and proud was I to have been a part of it. As others went to the mall, I went to the camp. As others went to the beach or made their usual drag from the laundry mat to the lake, I went to the camp. This became my preferred and intended destination, accessible only by boat....... or parachute.

I was often alone. No electricity, no phone, no traffic, just solitude. This is where my swamp life began. Four sets of bunk beds and an ol' barrel heater did host a multitude of visitors at times throughout the years. Uncountable stories are out there in fond memories of many a soul and some should stay there until the statute of limitations runs out.

For two decades it stood. For twenty years this well-built shack formed and had much influence on the outlook of life I hold today. The importance of silence, the necessity of self-reliance and self-audits. The appreciation of nature's beauty began here.

And for over two decades it's been gone, a result of the State and Corp of Engineers' unsurpassed wisdom in land management.

Thankful am I for the tutelage received under Mr. Frank's eye throughout this bargaining, assembling and building endeavor, for it has proved invaluable many times over in real life situations. Tis funny now looking back, how another man's dream helped to form my own.

Blind Date

When we first met, she was working a forty-hour midnight shift at the prison, taking a full fifteen-hour load at Gulf Coast Community College and competing on the pistol team. I knew she had grit, I liked that. I knew she could shoot, that bothered me some.

It began as a blind date. Well, so to speak. A mutual friend brought her over for supper one night, very casual. We shared a sparse home cooked meal, Gunsmoke on TV and sweet tea on the porch swing. Not much fanfare and I was hoping she wouldn't expect much. Seriously, how much could there be from a feller with a broke down truck, eight dollars in his pocket, two dogs for company and who showered outside by moonlight?

It went well enough I thought by night's end, we shook hands and they drove away. A coupla days later our mutual friend said she'd like to do it again. Hmm, I wondered what's wrong with this one. Surely an intelligent, pretty girl twelve years my junior could find something better to do on a Saturday night than hang out with the likes of me. But I dialed her up and she said ok.

I decided to take it up a notch and introduced her to the finest of curb-service dining at the Tally-Ho. Later, with milkshakes in hand we watched a sunset over East Bay. I could see right off that there was much potential standing next to me. And there it began, a courtship of four years.

Eventually she said, "I do" and that amazed me.

Long before the sun she rises. Coffee is ground, eggs sizzle, shirts are ironed, and socks are matched before my feet touch floor each morning. Cold frosty mornings will find her scraping ice from windshields after feeding our critters.

No one ever drew breath that anticipated and relished Motherhood more than she. It was embraced with every fiber of her being. She cherished the time of pregnancy; it was as if she felt honored to be so.

As the kids came, through the stories of Noah and Moses, Daniel and David, our children were exposed to and introduced to Christ at a young age, it was her primary goal of motherhood. She realized early on that most decisions have eternal consequences, and this was paramount. Still is.

She also saw to it that they knew Emily Dickinson and Robert Frost, Chopin and Wagner before they ever heard of Shania Twain or any Kardashian. I requested Poe and Willie Nelson but was flatly rejected.

They were also taught to fend for themselves early on. As soon as they were as tall as a laundry basket, they got acquainted with it. Twas the same for cast-iron and its correlation to the rumbling in their stomach. The apron strings were cut long before the knot even got tight. Motherhood in our house would be much akin to Maya Angelou's description of her own mother: "a hurricane in its perfect power. Or the climbing, falling colors of a rainbow."

Hard, difficult and trying times have arrived and camped on our doorstep many a time. It seems there have always been a pack of wolves circling our front door. Some wore suits and carried briefcases, most used the mailman to do their handiwork. She has always met them head on and never left or even backed up. She tries, I like that.

Tis my belief that a Mother's hands should be gentle and soothing and absorb tears. They should also be strong and swift. Every child should be able to look into a Mother's eyes in time of sorrow and find immediate comfort without question, without words. Children should also find correction in those same eyes with the same quickness. A Mother's voice should be one of encouragement and enlightenment, one that would draw a child in.

Blessed am I to have crossed paths with a genuine article. A few things have been learned along the way in watching firsthand this magic of Motherhood unfold.

No mother is perfect, some just try harder than others. And what is exposed on the outside does not a mother make. For "from the heart, the mouth speaks."

So Long, Ol' Friend

We met in the year of '01, she'd caught my eye from afar for she was young and strong and showed much promise. After a very brief courtship I brought her home to meet the family, immediate acceptance seemed to be the mutual response.

The past seventeen years have produced nothing short of a kindred bonding of the highest order. She assumed her position and responsibilities well and has always held up her end of the relationship. Countless hours we've spent together, there have been times of bounty and others of utter desolation. There were times when she ran on and on and on – other occasions she sat quiet and motionless as if to teach me a lesson of my neglect toward her.

Together we have endured many a thunderstorm, many a set-back and then there have been numerous majestic sunset strolls together enjoying God's creation.

Of late she had begun to complain of internal pains, and I took her to see a specialist yesterday. The diagnosis was bleak, imminent and ominous even. I stood aghast as the news was delivered so directly and without apology.

Today, it is with a degree of sadness I find myself alone with nothing but memories. My mind helplessly flutters trying to replay them all.

There is little one can do in times like this except sit in quietness, accept the decisions of her creator and remember the wonderful times shared together.

So-long family member and trusted companion of seventeen years. May you forever ripple the waters of the Great Beyond – the 1999 MotorGuide Great White trolling motor. Rest in Peace till we meet again.

The Bricks

Each child had a brick and a thin piece of linen. As the cold winds of December lashed the frosted, single pane windows of the ol' farmhouse, bricks were neatly placed by the fireplace before bedtime. Once warmed and wrapped in linen, three little sisters would scamper off to bed feeling grateful for their own brick. They would place them between their feet and hopefully fall fast asleep before their warmth subsided.

On this night, sleep seemed most elusive as wonderment and anticipation overrode a young girl's weariness - for this was Christmas Eve. Each child silently wondered: 'Would she like the doll, hand sewn from scraps of material and stuffed with hay? A length of rope for Daddy, woven from a mule's tail during stolen snatches of time between chores, would he like it when he sees it tomorrow? A painted rock from the creek bed for Mama and a new sage broom laced with lavender, surely that will fetch a smile. '

These sisters and their siblings soon to follow were influenced a touch different than most younguns of today. They were taught early on that finding happiness within themselves comes from the act of giving to others.

During their journey through adolescence, instilled in them was the fact that life on this earth is far too short to be lived dull or unappreciative of the creation that surrounds you. They would realize their greatest pleasures as they made those around them more comfortable in body and soul.

Gold, frankincense and myrrh were but forms of broom sage, mule hair and sack cloth to these children, for it was the sparkle in the eye of the recipient that brought their truest joy.

By many standards, rural life in the 1920's was hard. Even on Christmas, the livestock must be fed, eggs gathered and Ol' Florence's udders emptied before breakfast. For these little girls however, Christmas was a special day. It was a day of anticipation and excitement, a time of giggles and making cookies. After breakfast they would take turns reading passages from the book of Luke before opening their single gift.

Twas amongst these pages they learned of loving your neighbor as yourself and that the willingness to share does not make a person charitable – *it makes them free.*

And the most beautiful souls are those who can freely give without hesitation, without regret or fear of loss.

These often contend with the most pain – yet by far – live more happily in a single day than most live in a year. They learned that where there is withholding, there is insensitivity – there is callousness and those who build up walls of self-preservation can neither give nor receive. These are the souls of the dull.

Sisters three they were, and each became educators of young minds. Of a span of forty years or better they stood in a classroom with a chalkboard as a backdrop and passed on to youngsters what had been passed on to them.

Rarely do I back up to a fireplace without thinking of Mama's story of the bricks, of Christmas and the humbleness of its origins. For those in our charge, we find ourselves compelled with presenting the ideal gift. And while a flawless gift cannot be bought or wrapped it can be taught and instilled.

Hopefully, parents and teachers of today will choose to inspire within young minds that only by the giving of their talents will they ever receive more than they already have.

Lightning Bugs

Most nights before getting horizontal I make my way to the darkest corner of the yard to make sure The Big Dipper is still hanging where it should, and Little Bear remains in line. Except for the chirp of locusts and bellow of the frog in the pond it's a mighty quiet place and a few minutes there soothes my meager mind at day's end.

The past several weeks have found me searching for the final tell-tale sign of late Spring, the flashy frolic of the Lampyridae. Those in urban dwelling areas will refer to them as fireflies but if one is speakin or listenin in lower Wewahitchkan the denotation will be 'lightnin bug.' I truly enjoy the nights of late Spring here at the creek, especially the ones punctuated with the glittering glow of these magical lights.

Some twenty-five or so years back a young lady stopped by with a feisty two-year-old boy in tow. Twas my first introduction to a mini-tornado with legs and lungs. A strong-willed lad he was and his exercise of said appendages was most impressive. In short order I had to walk outside to elude the deafening roar for a minute and an epiphany was had.

It was one of those mystic nights when the lightning bugs were in a synchronized waltz, captivating almost. Taking the mason jar next to the water spigot and a towel from the clothesline – the stalk was on. In about two shakes a couple of these mesmerizing flights of light were performing their luminous dance in a jar.

Back inside I placed the tornado and the jar on the kitchen floor and turned off all the lights. It was darker'n two midnights in a jug. Immediately the sound of silence filled the house. No lullaby or medicine or duct tape needed - just nature's creation. I've never forgotten that night and it served as a delicate childhood reminder of chasing these flights of fancy around Ms. Rish's flower beds when this tornado was sent outside to spin down.

Jennifer brought one in the living room the other night, turned off the light and turned it loose. Much akin to the first honeysuckle bloom, the arrival of May flies and Catawba worms, the lightning bug is warmly greeted at our house.

Entertainment is fairly cheap as we are easily amused back here in the woods.

Long Beards 'n Leotards

I stood in the kitchen staring in utter disbelief at the calendar that hung inside the pantry door. It couldn't be right, it just couldn't. Beyond all measures there had been an egregious mistake, an obvious neglect of communication between the powers-that-be to have allowed a discrepancy of this magnitude. Far too late it was now to file an appeal.

On the one hand, 'the show must go on' and on the other 'Mother Nature waits on no one.' So what's a feller to do?

Today was Monday and the upcoming Saturday had been scheduled for my 4-year-old's second dance recital and this little girl was forevermore excited. The conflict arose because someone in the hierarchy of the Georgia Wildlife

Commission had failed to coordinate the opening day of Turkey Season with dance officials on the Florida side of the line.

The lack of consideration in matters such as these baffles me to this day.

After much discussion the wife and I worked out an amenable compromise that left everyone in a copacetic mood. The following Wednesday night was the dance rehearsal in full costume(s), and on that night the wife had to teach a children's class at the church. It was stipulated that I attend the rehearsal, thus getting the full effect... *and then some*, and she'd take care of the dance recital as I chased a long-beard around in the woods on a south Georgia farm come Saturday morning. Fair enough I thought.

There I sat in the dark auditorium with my young pullet at hand and another 200 young girls with their mothers, their grandmothers, every aunt they laid claim to, their sisters, friends of their sisters, the head waitress at the coffee shop, and all other estrogen-infused life forms in a three-county area.

And then there was me.

Remain calm, adapt, and persevere towards a satisfactory conclusion has been an ongoing life lesson Jennifer and I have tried to instill in our children. Teaching this philosophy while replacing a bicycle chain or removing a well-set hook from a flopping catfish was much simpler than the situation I was now belly-button deep in.

The shrieks and squeals and mayhem that every other person in the place appeared to relish, even thrive in, shattered, then set aflame every hair and nerve ending in my body.

True enough there were moments of unexpected kindness as my obvious lack of skills was noticed by several onlookers. They kindly offered their assistance with the tying of a bow (apparently a bowline knot is unacceptable in dance competition) or the helping with leotards and ribbons and such.

The joy I felt came solely from watching my daughter twirl and giggle with delight. I tried to match her smile for smile and to apply the rouge and glitter just so.

It is my belief that she, even at a tender age, understood her daddy was completely out of his element. But he was there nonetheless, standing amongst the swirling chaos holding his daughter's tiny hand on one side and holding a pink frilly bag in the other.

The Whole World on a Shelf

"**D**addy what's the difference between La Niña and El Niño? And why does......" I silently interrupted, raising my finger to my lips and eagerly passed on the identical response I received countless times under Mama's instruction, "Go look it up."

We lived in the middle of town back then tween Main and Back Street, I was six or maybe seven and was sitting in the corner while my butt cooled off from the latest infraction when someone knocked on the door. "Ma-maaaa, somebody's at the door." "Then wipe your face and see who it is." Glad to get up, I opened the door and a feller stood there with a satchel in one hand and his hat in the other. "Hello young man, who's doing that singing I hear?" "That'd be Mr. Poley next door, he gets tuned up bout this time of day." "Is your Mama or Daddy home?"

About a month later they arrived, and Daddy built a wooden shelf to put them on. The traveling Encyclopedia salesman had done his job and now the world was at our fingertips complete with picture in living color. Mama was so proud.

Homework assignments came later in school. A topic was given, five hundred words were required complete with source, author, page number, footnotes, etc. etc. The purpose here was simply that time and effort translates to learning. An afternoon or two had to be set aside to go to the library to obtain these resources to complete the task. This took time and meant no marble shootin, no bike ridin or in later years, no meetin your squeeze at the lake until the homework was done, especially those of us who lived under the same roof with a schoolteacher.

"Look it up." It has a much different significance today. Press a button and it's on a screen immediately in the palm of your hand, press another and a printout shoots out from somewhere and 'vwa - la' there it is. In less time than it took me to build a fried bologna sandwich my daughter had the entire sea current patterns of the South Pacific, wind shear projections and rainfall estimates for the next two years in her hands. "Hum, that's interesting" was her response. I stood aghast.

I remember spending two weeks day and night it seems putting together a paper and speech for Ms. Kelley on the rise and fall of the water levels at Jim Woodruff Dam during the barge traffic years in high school. I remember it to this today. All my daughter can muster is a faint "Hum, that's interesting."

Yesterday, now 50 years later, I stood looking at those Encyclopedias still on the shelf and wondered what to do with them.

From Where I Sit

The damp wooden boards were milled long ago in an ol' shaded wood shop by the lake. They were cut into slats, dried, then sanded and assembled with a specific purpose in mind. Daddy had an old-school way of doing things when it came to woodworking. He was always covered in sawdust, it clung to him like glitter to a pole dancer.

I lent a hand in the making of this particular porch swing. "Who's this one for daddy?" "Oh, a good friend of mine needs one." Sturdy it was and comfortable too, at least one attribute you'd expect from dead-head cypress.

Several weeks later, I moved back to Wewa and settled into this tiny house back here in the woods. I could hear Daddy's ol' truck rattling one afternoon as he pulled into the yard. He said he needed help with the swing again. This time to hang it for a good friend that needed one. It still hangs and I still sit.

There's an ol' Adirondack chair also hand-made, a distant second cousin to the swing, it faces west usually with a towel hanging across its back. A store-bought rocking chair idles beside the swing and like me, it's weathered with time. An aging barber chair stands there too, I occupy it every other Sunday afternoon.

A small shelf just big enough for a cat to sit is attached to the corner post. It's just high enough the dogs can't interrupt their persnickety eating habits. In the other corner is the shower, from which all blessings flow.

Twenty-four years here this month and so much has changed. Much has not. There have been times of sorrow and disappointment, moments of jubilation and many instances of uncertainty have shared their season on these boards. The slow rock of the chair and gentle sway of the swing have often served as pleasant company for a searching mind.

Gains and losses on the incomprehensible subjects of life, death, eternity and the next willow-fly hatch have rendered themselves here. Why, I often wonder, isn't gender identification as simple as taking a peek? Why isn't Tupelo real Tupelo anymore and why oh why do young lives end and old lives linger?

From where I sit the views of man are innumerable. Peace and agony seems to be offered here in equal portion. A feller can choose to sit and mull over issues far beyond his control or he can take solace in the satisfaction knowing he did his best today. I believe each necessitates a place in a man's heart.

Enough black coffee, sweet tea and sweat from a hoe handle have been poured here to float the USS Nimitz. Dogs have dreamed belly up in the flower bed below and so have I, pondered much and prayed often. The Almighty spends a lot of time in the swing too.

A sundry of sunrises and sunsets have been beheld here, along with clear starry nights and cold rainy days. It is here the pains and injustices of the day are released on the evening breeze. It is also here the opportunities of early mornings are anticipated.

From here one notices the hanging of the moon and how utterly unaffected it is by the goings-on raging below it.

Long ago a gentle man began milling some damp cypress slats in a shady shop by the lake. He had no idea of the influence they would one day have……. or perhaps he did.

Moses

I said nope, we don't need another one; we have two at home now. It ain't happenin.

It was early July and hotter than a jalapeño fart. Me n Jennifer had ventured north to the happenin town of Wausau to the annual Possum Festival. A long-standing local event that neither of us had had the experience of attending.

My wife was anxious to try her luck with her soap and candle wares. I just happened to be in tow and provided muscle setting up.

With tent up, signs and displays arranged, tables and jars neatly in order, the sweat rolled freely. No sooner had I found a shady spot and a glass of tea than a tall young lady sidles up next to my wife with a cardboard box full of cuddling puppies. Aawww, ain't they cute and they're cheap.

"Thanks, but not today."

My wife is Ellie Mae Clampett at heart and will take in any and all stray critters found in the northern hemisphere. The bonier, the sadder and more downtrodden, the better it seems. Rabbits and birds, armadillos or alligators, it matters not.

I knew the only attached addendum of responsibility on my behalf would be to work more overtime to afford feed for this menagerie of critters.

Hours later, as the festival was winding down, the lady strolls by again and stops. "I only have one left and he's the runt," paying me no mind and looking directly at my wife. I recognized the look; I'd seen it before.

I'd grown quite fond of hot meals and clean socks so on the way home we named him Moses.

Only a brief period of time has there been in my life when I didn't have a hound of some sort around the house. Too many, way too many for me to recollect. Some came by design and with a purpose, others simply arrived seeking shelter. Some came and took up residence, others came, then vanished in the night. I remember one we aptly dubbed 'Not Long.'

Like children and adults, each animal possesses attributes and personalities that help to make our temporary existence on this earth much more pleasant.

Moses and maybe one other have stood head and shoulders above the rest. He was a Lab/American bulldog mix and fit in immediately. He grew strong and guarded our property with a vengeance. And yet would go belly up for a child's attention.

Moses spent seven long, peaceful years living a life of quality. He enjoyed plenty of shade, cool water and ate better than most. Moses was family. He displayed emotion like I have never witnessed in any animal: joy, guilt, sadness, love, and at times, pure unadulterated excitement. He was just like a child in many respects – and a full-grown bear in others.

Like a well-disciplined century, he made noise when appropriate and was stealthily quiet most of the time. Moses was as much a fixture on our porch as was the rocking chair. In fact, he spent his share of time in it.

We laid him to rest today, found him in his favorite spot. I've dug many a hole over the years for many a critter but none as deep as this one.

Chicken Talk

For decades now I haven't listened to the radio in the truck and if it wasn't for a missing knob it would be considered in 'primo' condition. The strum of the tires and the whistling wind from a door that seldom shuts properly has provided enough melody for me.

I don't really know when it began but at some point, the sound of silence beckoned my attention. Oh, dear heavenly Father, Mary mother of God, grits and all things sacred, do I adore the sound of silence.

In a world filled with ceaseless noise we attempt to exist. Aside from basic and necessary communication required, this fat boy much prefers the little quiet time that is afforded him. I say quiet time because I have never really discovered true silence.

Stood have I in a rain forest in Central America during the monsoon, climbed trees in remote parts of Canada as snow fell, been stranded in the woods on the outskirts of Bogalusa, La. for a day and a night. No true silence to be found. Mother Nature doesn't allow it, for there is always a rustle in the leaves, a groaning in the trees or the distant roll of thunder. One must only close their eyes to hear it.

Our quietest spot is often the back porch, a half mile to the highway, a quarter mile to our closest neighbor. And they're as quiet as mice peeing on a cotton ball.

I was reminiscing about a back porch event six or seven years ago that duly changed my daily conversations. I had been busier than the paper shredders in Hillary's office and had retired to the porch seeking solitude. There sat Henrietta, one of our free-range chickens, perched atop the weight bench. Sleeping at her feet was Moses, our trusted watch dog. The very same dog that refused to even tolerate the intrusion of a shadow into his domain. *Hmm.....*

Well Henrietta, you must really have something on Moses for him to allow this. "Bak-bak" "Henrietta, did you sleep well?" "Cluck." "Anything go on out here last night that I need to know about?" *Silence.* "You see that single gardenia bloom over there this late in the year, what do you think that means?" "Bak-bak." "Have you ever marveled at the equation of Pi?" "Cluck." "What about the Pythagorean theorem? Aren't triangles interesting or do you prefer oval shapes?" *Silence.*

"Do you believe there is a direct correlation tween the vast and rapid expanse of technology with the apparent diminished communication skills of this generation?" "Cluck, bak-bak." "Living side by side with the rabbits, an entirely different species, combined with a wandering, domineering dog in your neighborhood, y'all still remain friends. How do you do it?" "Bak-bak-bak."

I sensed immediately there was much more to this bird than a simple egg layer. There was an aged wisdom in those beady eyes. And she had somehow conquered what all the forces of nature up til now could not: apparent dominion over an eighty-pound bulldog. I was indeed intrigued.

"Henrietta, what's your opinion on the current administration in the White House?" She did an about-face, lifted her tail feathers, and now I must go get the bleach and a garden hose.

Today was my first conversation with a chicken, but somehow knew it wouldn't be my last.

The Barn

My last conversation with Mama was about barns.

It was my weekend watch, and she was in bed when I arrived mid-afternoon. Refused did I to allow her stay there. We'd just made it down the hall to her favorite chair when she suddenly wanted to sit out on the porch. Sat quietly at first she did, her eyes darting to and fro around the yard, to the water's edge and across the lake. Finally, she seemed to focus on the shed on the west side of the property.

"Son, where's Robert?"

He's not here right now Mama. I felt no need to remind her Daddy left this world twenty years earlier.

"Well, it's not like him to leave the barn in disarray. When will he be back?

She was quiet again, but I could see the wheels turning and I relished this. Sitting there in the rocking chair, I recalled a story she'd once written and submitted to the Jackson County historical group. The story was about her family's barn along Highway 69 in Grand Ridge. Her rendition was laced with honor and pride, struggle and craftsmanship, survival and anger.

It was a story of a man's word and the value of keeping it.... regardless of the cost.

As her published story reflected decades earlier, for farming families living off the land in the 1920's the barn was the focal point of their existence. The house was simply a structure you exited at sunrise to begin your day and a place you gathered for the evening meal, conversation, and a night's rest. Twas The Barn from which all life flowed. It housed and protected the oxen, the horses, and Ol' Florence the milk cow. It stored the grain and hay that fed them and the chickens that, in turn, fed the family. The barn was of paramount importance. Anvils and axes, plows and ropes, and other implements of destruction were stored there. Often it was a man's only source of shade and solitude.

"Son, does the roof leak?"

Only when it rains, Mama.

Her eyes of ninety-five years, still blue and cutting when they needed to be, for Mama never did cotton to sarcasm. It was here her countenance changed and yet another Ecclesiastical lesson was rendered. "After you fix the leak and straighten up out there, make sure none of the tools are damaged inside. If so, get them in working order. And if there is anything the neighbors need, you let them borrow it. Not all of our neighbors have a barn, so they'll be needing some things from time to time. And you let them have whatever they need, you hear. Son, to have good neighbors – you have to be one."

I will, Mama.

"I'm not sure when your daddy'll be back, but you need to get started out there right now, you never know when the next storm will come."

One would hope our final conversation with a loved one would reveal some ancient secret, some nugget of timeless wisdom, or a life-altering philosophical tidbit of advice that guides a yearning soul to a point of solace.......... *now looking back, I believe it did.*

A Good Neighbor

There he sat, under his barn.

I was hurriedly making the corner on my way home to a well-deserved glass of lemonade. I had just pulled a ten-hour shift dealing with heat, handcuffs and attitude. My commute is about thirty minutes and normally that is enough to mentally de-frag from a day such as this. I felt a profound need for some quiet time and to feel Mama's ol' oscillating fan blowing up my britches leg. I was less'n a hundred yards from my mailbox when I saw him.

Looking out across a freshly plowed field sat Larry Kemp, the epitome of a good neighbor. He is extremely watchful and observant in his neighborhood. Quiet, minds his own business yet helpful beyond measure and always, always in a good mood. I like Larry. So I pulled up next to the barn. "Get out'n set down a spell." I did.

This scene has played out numerous times over the years under his shed or mine. I sat down on a five-gallon bucket and leaned against a John Deere tractor that's seen more action than the Tally-Ho on a Saturday night. Larry looked tired today and should have. He'd just finished planting twelve rows of sweet corn with a push plow, Silver Queen. I wondered why, because he didn't usually waste time on sweet corn.

There's much to be said at the end of a day when a feller has accomplished a nasty but necessary task. Mostly what's said is exhaustion. We sat, we spat, we enjoyed the shade and mixed aroma of diesel fuel and honeysuckle.

We discussed okra's need for heat and how tomatoes benefit greatly from a good dose of Epsom salt just as we do. Larry is not the least bit shy of dropping a corn seed in the ground, mostly field corn as the numerous rows and a rebuilt Covington two row planter will attest to.

Dixie 18, Yella Dent and Trucker's Favorite are etched into Larry's DNA. He loves to break ground and tend it. He takes much delight in what it will yield, but his greatest joy I believe is being able to drop off a mess of produce to a needy soul. Many times, I've arrived home to find a melon or two and a bucket of okra on the porch. No note attached nor none needed to know where it came from.

We spoke of a hard day's work and how they never seem to end. At length we talked of planting seeds and the nutrients needed for sustaining a healthy life. Larry talked of how futile all of our efforts are if we fail to take strong measures in keeping the varmints outa our gardens. He began speaking of raising purple hull peas versus browsing deer. He talked of growing and tending to watermelons, trying to get them to maturity and how the coyotes can destroy them overnight. He spoke in farming terms, but I think he was trying to teach me something else.

Midway through our second chew, I reminded him of giving my boy his first haircut when he was about a year old. And how he'd not had a store-bought haircut since, now seventeen years later. He managed a wry grin and his tired eyes seemed to glisten a bit as he began recalling memories of his barber shop days.

Leaning back in his chair, Larry switched gears and spoke of flat-top haircuts and how not everyone could wear one. He could still recall by name all of those who did..... and still do. Like the field corn, I believe flat-top haircuts were his favorite and took much pride in getting them 'just right.' We reminisced about Uncle Preacher and the mirrors on both walls of the barber shop. How it seemed one could gaze forever in those endless reflections. This imagery gave way to much provocative thought to a young lad.

A hot towel, lather and a straight razor were tools of his craft. How rarely they are used today. A lost art so to speak. As a young lad of the early seventies I never relished getting a haircut, but had a standing, mandatory appointment every other week whether I wanted one or not. What I did look forward to was the conversation. Not that I understood it all at nine years old, and though the men usually kept their musings 'kid friendly', I quickly learned to read between the lines. There is an education to be had in the barber shop.

It'd only been twenty minutes or so but we'd both drifted back to pleasant times. Good conversation with a good neighbor can do a body wonders. In no time the aggravations of a long day of razor wire and felonious actions had evaporated into thin air.

Many a man can amass many things on this earth, some can stack up more money than a show pony can jump over, but a man with a good neighbor is the most blessed.

Facing My Demons

Comes a time we must all face our demons, eye to eye and nose to nose. Necessary it is to make positive changes that affect our mind, body, and soul in order to move forward. New year, new beginning so to speak. Personally, I've had a degree of difficulty of late in areas of expression, unable to focus, gather and arrange thoughts and get them on paper - which is my purest form of release.

Those who know me are aware of this extended state of melancholy amongst other issues. A clean slate is vitally needed and must begin with me.

A cleansed heart; fresh air in the lungs, clear eyes to see the true beauty that surrounds us is a necessity in living happily and abundantly.

Being totally honest with yourself, your family, and others is equally important. Having always tried to instill this trait in my younguns I have found myself in a major dilemma. Well-versed am I in the importance of admittance, of asking forgiveness and the payment of penance.

Maybe this isn't the best format to reveal secrets, but after lengthy discussions, much crying and much prayer with Jennifer we think it best to get the truth out and begin anew. Grateful am I to God that she still stands beside me and is willing to help.

I've had discretions over the years, some dalliances going back decades. Hard to believe at this stage of life. Yet, there she was, always around and willing to go. I knew better and she didn't care. We all have our demons, some public, and some closet.

Many times, I fought the temptation, many times I lost, and twice or eight times I have begged forgiveness. A few times it became a ménage – ha, at my age. There is many a life lesson to be learned here, that anything is possible for anyone given the right circumstance, especially if we are weak.

Blessed am I to have an understanding, supportive wife and forgiving God in difficult times. The cards are now on the table and this story told, my relationships with Sara Lee and Lil Debbie are over and a new chapter of life can begin.

Bea Bea Bugs

He handed her a piece of Tupelo root, it was as big as her arm. She turned and said, "Daddy it's so light, it could float away." The feller smiled with approval and replied, "That's the point. Come in here, young lady, and watch what happens."

The room was dusty but neat. Obvious was the fact that much work had been underway. Everything had a place and a reason why. When one man enters another man's shed......... you notice things. One, you're just honored to be granted admittance into his sanctuary, and two, you'll prolly see something that will improve your own.

Now this feller'd be the first to admit that he didn't make the short list for the next Southern Living Garden Exposé, but what comes outa his shed is truly a work of art.

At one station he cut and drilled holes in the Tupelo root, at another he delicately sanded what Mother Nature took a myriad of seasons to produce. As he held the small piece of wood to the light for inspection, I wondered how many storms and floods had it endured, how many shellcracker had nestled next to it? And now, how many would be caught because of it?

Quiet and enthralled, she listened as he explained the next steps of cutting and gluing, more sanding then painting these tiny individual pieces. In front of a work bench he sat, an exhaust fan strategically placed - homemade ingenuity that would allow multiple applications of paint was further evidence that necessity is still the mother of invention.

It was then he said, "Let's go inside and I'll show you the rest." Much akin to just finishing off a heaping plate of fried chicken, fried okra and taters n gravy – then to find out there is dessert too. "Daddy there's more?"

We followed him up the steps, Rascal the wonder hound barking every breath. He takes his job as guard and protector very serious.

In yet another room that it would take a body a lifetime to sort through, the finish work began. Drawers upon drawers, shelves stuffed with feathers of every type imaginable. The colors and designs seemed endless as did the possibilities of a unique product. Needles and thimbles, twine and glue were everywhere.

He talked and told stories along the way and she soaked them in. As he made his last wrap of the twine and final snip of the scissors a small plastic bag was slipped over the unique, hand-crafted fly and handed her the finished product. "Now don't tell the Chinese what you've seen here today young lady. They've got satellites trying to steal this technology." She smiled and gave him a hug and promised not to tell.

At this moment I realized my parenting obligations were near complete in arranging this introduction. An hour earlier I'd met my daughter in town to assist her with a 'growing-up endeavor.' It was then we drove north, then east down a lonesome road into a neat yard nestled quietly next to the Dead Lakes.

In a rocking chair on the front porch he sat. "Is that him, Daddy?" Yep, that's John Chambliss in the flesh – prepare yourself.

Mother's Day 'n May Flies

Two life-long friends were traveling far and at considerable expense to enjoy a day or so in our version of paradise. The white-tail rut is now a distant memory and the gobbling of the birds had run its course. Dan Powell from the shore of the Atlantic at Fernandina Beach and inland from Gainesville Frank Graddy came. The May flies were hatching from the Dead Lakes to Saul's Creek and these fellas wanted in on it.

The aforementioned expense came in this form: Today was the birthday of one fella's wife and the wedding anniversary of the other, all wrapped together on Mother's Day weekend……….. and still they came.

Preliminary preparations began a month ago for me and the stacking up of brownie points for them. A lot of yes-ma'ams said gingerly and an extensive list of questionable honey-dos were completed quickly, quietly and without question. Feet were rubbed, errands ran and conversations were listened to intently.

Arrangements had been made, steaks bought, fish cookers ready and forgiveness asked in advanced. The hatching of the flies waits for no one.

A few years back a coupla guys made it their mission to collect data and predict the willow fly hatch along our river system. They bought gadgets and tested water temperature on a daily basis. They recorded barometric pressures and moon phases. They wrote down rainfall amounts and humidity levels and factored them into their equation for several years in a row. They analyzed tree bark and water clarity, took pictures of Tupelo blooms, cloud formations, and willow leaves. All in attempts to be standing on the bow with rod in hand when the magic hour of the hatch rendered itself.

After four years of research they came to this conclusion: they'll hatch whenever they want to. Heck, if they'd simply listened to Bo John Lester years ago, they could have been standing ready within a forty-eight-hour window and knew where to go.

Not a soul at Iola Landing when I arrived this morning, not even the sun. This was a good sign. I just wanted to make some rounds and do some scouting for my friends so their trip would be worth it when they returned home to face their wives.

I backed the boat in and started back up the ramp, a slight miscalculation and the back tires went down. Stuck again. Only the 223,458th time in my life. Charles Nunnery showed up and pulled me out, a good man he is. Another feller grabbed my bow rope and pulled the boat in, colliding it with my trailer light; I hope they sell them in singles.

On the way back down the ramp I slipped in the mud and busted my behind and wrenched my fly-flipping hand. This current position brought me eye level with the gunwale of the boat. It was here I noticed the registration had expired a month ago. And so it is in the life of a Brown.

Determined and undeterred I proceeded forth. I turned the key and the usually dependable outboard just sputtered, as if to openly mock my good intentions. It sputtered again to make its position clear. I thought it may be a simple fix and knew I had the means at hand to get it running. Oh but no. The emergency toolbox that hasn't moved since 2001 was nowhere to be found, not even a screwdriver nor a match to burn it with.

Frustration and futility often arrive arm in arm and long ago I learned not to square off with them when they team upon you. I loaded the boat, made sure I had a spare tire and headed home. These boys were on their own.

A Day with Beau

It was early spring, and week's end was approaching with a quickness, yet couldn't seem to get here fast enough. The past month at work had been more trying than usual. For anyone working behind the wire in a prison, a good day is defined simply as 'going home alive.'

A coupla days off were due me, and we'd planned a short jaunt away from home to allow the mind to unwind and refocus. The lack of digits in my bank account prevented distant travel and our ability to eat too high up on the hog. This meant rescheduling the trip to watch the Swallows return to Capistrano and now, more than likely Vienna Sausages and crackers would be on the menu for the next few days.

The hunting cabin in South Georgia was our initial intended destination, but at crunch time no one really wanted to make the two-hour drive. Twas here that my wife suggested that Beau and I go to Mama's house on the lake and camp out. On short reflection, it proved to be a grand idea.

Mama had crossed over Jordan about a year earlier, and her house on the lake sat vacant. Well, vacant of flesh and blood, my siblings and I hadn't gotten around to cleaning out a lifetime of accumulation yet. The house was still fully functional, and the back-porch view was always spectacular.

Beau and I decided to hide the truck behind the shed, turn our phones off, unload the tackle boxes and let nature take its course.

Daylight found me where Daddy used to sit, in a homemade swing on the porch. The lake this morning was as a huge mirror, reflecting the bottom of heaven. Fog rose slowly around the lake's edge where the mallards splash and play.

Beau wasn't far behind and was making his way down the hill to the lake. Reels and rods, copious amounts of tackle and with a smidgeon of determination, he prepared to cast off.

I sat and watched and imagined how often my daddy must have watched his sons make this same walk to the lake from this exact spot. He loved every inch of this place and what it represents. I realized now that it had brought him as much fulfilment as it did me watching my son now do the same.

I'd stepped inside to get another cup when I heard him hollerin, "Daadd-deeey, GET THE NET!!"

He was standing flatfooted on the dock with his rod tip bent toward the south, and he was holding on for dear life.

I don't move as fast as I used to but got there in time to enjoy the show. Right off you could tell it was a biggun, but it hadn't broke water yet so we weren't sure how big.

"Son, keep your rod tip up and let him wear himself out. As long as he don't head for the grass – let him go. Keep the rod up and adjust the drag to slow him down a bit, just hold on. Don't get in a hurry, we have all day and this one is worth it."

I turned around to see if it was my Daddy giving these instructions. No one was visible, but he was there. There looking over my shoulder, grinning his approval and whispering the now familiar instructions that hadn't been uttered in forty years.

The big bucket-mouth bass finally broke water and tried to shake the hook, Beau held firm though I know his butt puckered a bit because mine did. Twas here the show really began, this one was big!

Finally, Beau was able to guide this ol' monster into the waiting net, and we got her on the dock. We had no scales, but I found a length of Mama's sewing tape in the pantry. Twenty-seven inches long and a girth of twenty-two and five-eighth inches. Whew, a big female laden with eggs. We turned a phone on and took a few pictures for posterity.

Fifty years of diligent fishing and never have I landed one such as this. I immediately began thinking of starting a revolving charge account at the taxidermist when I heard a splash at lake's edge.

There stood Beau grinning and empty handed. 'Daddy, I let her go, she was about to lay eggs, and the battle was enough for me."

My daddy was doubly proud this day. I could hear him whispering to me again, "Son, you don't need to travel far and wide to bond and make memories. You just need to be content wherever you are with whatever you have. Just spend time together and let nature take its course."

Our Most Precious Commodity

Looking back we can plainly see that there was an element in our young lives that we once considered limitless, and we held no knowledge of its value or importance. As young lads and lasses, the weeks leading up to our birthdays or the last day of school and the Mother of them all – Christmas – brought this element to a snail's pace even though we willed and wished it forward with fevered urgency.

Today, just as it was then and for millennia before, we begin to realize this element cannot be bought or sold at any price, neither harnessed nor grasped nor held no matter the firmness of our grip. Ever in motion, it waits not for the king nor does it tarry for the pauper, yet every soul drawing breath is granted a brief audience into its court.

Each of us is offered a portion of it to do with as we deem appropriate. For some fame, others fortune. Some devote their allotment to king and country while others pledge it to one fleeting cause or another that seems relevant at the time. There's a measure of folks that dedicate their unknown share full-tilt boogie in pursuit of pleasure at any cost having been taught that we only live once.

Truly blessed are those who recognize its genuine value early in life and learn to view their allotted portion as a gift... treat it with respect and use it as God intended, a means and a tool to provide love, comfort and laughter to everyone they encounter.

A truth we are taught in the book of James is: "Yet, you do not know what tomorrow will bring, What is your life? For you are but a vapor that appears for a little while and then vanishes."

Many, like me, don't catch on so quick and fail to see it until later in years. If we simply viewed our lives as the flash of a firefly at night, the breath of a whitetail in winter or a shadow that dances across a field and fades at sunset, we might choose to do things differently. To live each day deliberately and with purpose. To treat the days ahead with more respect than the days behind.

It matters not if we have fought lions, wrestled bears, saved the rain forest or stacked up more money than a show dog can jump over. If we cannot look back at the end of it all and have not given quality *time* to our own family and friends what have we really accomplished?.............. There it is..... TIME, always has been and will forevermore be, the most precious element known to man.

We tend to interpret 'pursuit of happiness' as a pay-off at the end of a long-fought battle, or complete solace culminating only at the end of an agonizing journey. We often miss the timely joys in the chosen moments each day brings because of our lack of awareness of the simple things that constantly surround us.

I wonder... does retirement or complete success in our chosen endeavors define true happiness? Does the wealth we strive for cost us our health prohibiting our enjoyment of it in the end?

Do the opportunities we furnish our children provide them an esteemed degree and yet fail them in the fundamental values of integrity and humanity?

I was told once that our families will only be as strong as the amount of quality time we invest in them. So often there seems precious little of it to go around (hence, it's preciousness). We spend it running to n fro, barely stopping to scratch our own butt struggling to do all.

Ben Franklin said, "Time is the stuff life is made of, don't squander it." For those who *wait* time is painfully slow, for those who live in *fear* time is swift, for those who *grieve* time tends to drag on – but for those who find *peace* and *love* in their soul, time is an eternity...

Piddlin

Today begins a coupla days off and though it began at three in the a.m., it began nonetheless. The younguns have now departed to church camp and Jennifer has a few obligations of which I am not involved. This leaves me some precious time to practice, maybe even enhance my favorite craft.

Many crafts I learned from my daddy, the presentation of a fly to a bream under a lily pad and the ability to read the grain in a hardwood board and make it into something perty. I learned some other stuff too.

He spent most of his days clad in overalls and in one hand was a hammer, a fishin pole or a garden hoe. He was very proficient with each. He could talk to a stranger with ease and read every word Louis L'amour ever wrote. At the top of his many talents though was the highly revered craft of 'piddling'. At this, he was a master.

A coupla things one must know about piddlin, and I learned it early on – piddlin ain't work nor was it ever intended to be. There is to be no sweat involved in the fine art of piddlin. If sweat is involved, then it ain't piddlin. No heavy tools such as grinders or chain hoists are allowed.

However, anything involving a yella handle Case knife, a stick of wood or a rocking chair qualifies as essentials.

If you were to repair a weed eater during high grass in June, that my friend, is considered work. But to replace a gasket on the same weed eater in late December is simply 'piddlin'.

Granted it may become necessary to fix the rung on a deer stand during the white-tail rut, this is strictly forbidden under the guidelines of 'pure piddlin' and harsh penalties may be imposed.

Those considering the craft must understand that neither hunting nor fishing nor a round of golf qualifies as piddling. Each of the aforementioned requires planning and a direct action, disqualifying you from the realm of piddlin.

One does not plan to piddle, it just happens. You can't set out to piddle; you have to just linger into it.

I asked a feller a while back at breakfast what he was planning to do that day, he said, "Absolutely nothing, I ain't doing nothing today — and I ain't even gone start doin that till around noon."

It is worth noting that there is a colossal difference between laziness and piddlin. Laziness and piddlin are from two different planets.

The whole idea here is to pass time without wasting time and to be able to do it without any regret. I'm of the belief that there should be a complete doctrine written on the craft of piddlin.

Fully aware am I that not everyone's DNA will allow them to willingly participate, which is probably why God at the last minute erased the eleventh commandment – "Thou shalt piddle." But for those of us who can fully embrace this art, it is an honor to uphold.

Cuteness 'n Carnage

Outside in the darkness I hear the puppies growling and scurrying across the porch; it sounds like a fierce game of tug-of-war. Probably with one of my new work boots or the new towel left draped over the rocking chair. As part of me tightens up and reaches for the broom handle, I think of my Mama and sit back down. How many times she must have felt the same way with me. I close my eyes and try not to imagine what I'll find in the yard when the sun comes up an hour from now – or more importantly.......what I won't.

I stepped over a half-chewed, now non-functional life jacket by the front door last night and the poncho liner that's been missing for a month was right next to it. All compliments of Bella and company. Atticus, our Lab puppy, is about eight months old and two of his nieces, Bella and Mildred, have trod this yard for half that long. Two of them are quite tolerable when left to themselves, tis when they combine their efforts that destruction is inevitable. The one we call Bella, however, possesses a rare trait of confidence for her age. She has a fearless, take-charge, I don't need you, I'll do it myself attitude. She'll lead armies one day.

Trying to count the critters I have shared space with would be like trying to count the rolled joints at a Willie Nelson concert. Dogs and cats of various breeds, rabbits and quail by the dozens, turkey and chickens have all taken up residence here. For the most part they are pleasant to be around and, like Willie, have a soothing effect on the body, and I need that nowadays.

I cannot say by most folks' standards that our critters are pampered very much. They are fed from the bag and the table alike. Watered from the bowl or the pond at their choosing, they're given shelter, scratched on the head, played with and talked to. And Jennifer did bring them in a coupla nights last week when the mercury touched the teens and bedded them by the fireplace. I had no say in this matter.

This diversity of critters adds a magical element to life that I find most amusing at times. For me it is free entertainment with a front row seat. As the cats respect the chickens and the chickens tolerate the new puppies, a continuous show is performed in our back yard.

Kinda like the elementary schoolyard antics at recess when Mr. Rouse insisted upon putting on the boxing gloves when two boys crossed the line. "Your rights end at another man's nose," he used to say, "now deal with it." With a quickness a boy learned to be mindful of another's space and also to be well prepared to defend his own.

In past years this puppy stage was the most trying for me and my patience was not a virtue to behold. Twas much akin to havin a yard full of two-year-old younguns hyped up on cotton candy or using a blender with the lid off.

I've gotten better, more tolerant it seems or maybe it's quite possibly that I'm just simply viewing life from new eyes.

Now that the sun is up it's time to stroll the yard, survey the puppy carnage and clean it up.

On the bright side, at least I now know where the poncho is, and rain's a comin.

Will It Really Matter in a Hunerd Years?

Will it really matter in a hunerd years?

Got outa bed early on Saturday with no pressing engagements in mind, nor any obligations to kith or kin that I could recall. From daylight to dark today was mine. This did much to soothe my mental status before feet touched floor.

The trip from bed to porch went smoother and quieter than usual and the only embarrassing fact was that the sun was there waiting on me. I'd waited all week for this chance to catch up, had laid out tools in advance and had an itinerary in mind.

From my vantage point I could see two acres of belly button high grass that need bush-hogging, forty yards of fencerow that begged attention and the right front tire on the mower was flat. I dearly hope the two on the boat trailer get me to the landing as soon as word of the first hatch arrives.

The purple martins have been here for over a month and the birdhouse is still under the bench, sad. Haven't had water to the kitchen sink for ten days now and the oil and filter that need changing have been in the truck so long it's probably expired.

Scattered about the yard and well beyond were the remnants of the joyous destruction of a chocolate lab puppy. I didn't need those shoes anymore, I guess. The field is plowed but nary a seed in the ground, tomato plants are still in the buckets. And..................

Only thirty seconds had elapsed, and I had to close my eyes to make it all stop. I was truly surprised at what happened next.

Focusing on nothing except the back of my eyelids - the jasmine and honeysuckle along the fence row were now detectable thanks to a southerly breeze.

This alone soothed the soul. The echoing of the whippowills back along the tree line melding with dancing windchimes and a croaking frog in the pond produced a three-part harmony only the splendor of nature could render...

In less time than it takes a fat baby to poot, the building pressure of the undone chores at hand had faded.

I guess what daddy said was true, "Son you're lookin, but you ain't seein." Sometimes you gotta close your eyes to enjoy the wonders around you.

It was right about then that a coupla waffles arrived, topped with two runny eggs and a cup of coffee.

Scout, our new puppy sat anxiously lickin her lips, eyes fixed intently on the plate but didn't make a sound. This one has potential. Time spent with a puppy is time well spent, and now she has a thing for eggs and Tupelo.

And I have a thing for a rocking chair, black coffee and a cool breeze. *I think I'll just sit a spell*......... what will it all matter in a hunerd years anyway....

Watchin Each Other

He's been sitting there for twenty minutes now. I noticed him on my initial scan of the backyard, he's prolly been waitin there much longer. About a dozen fence posts down from the corner he sits motionless.

It's a red-tailed hawk best I can tell and not a very big one. Certainly, he was aware of my presence long before I was of his. I'm slipping a bit in those areas of stealth and finesse, not to mention the ruckus the puppies made the minute I sat down in the swing.

The sky is grey this morning and a damp mist hangs between me and the wood-line. The mercury called for a sleeve after first light but now a south breeze tells me its need will be short lived.

The tiny pasture on which he sits is covered in dead knee-high grass, so is the acre behind him and the one to the south. With the exception of the occasional scamper of the puppies it is an eerily quiet and still winter morning.

His patience and discipline atop the chosen fence post are impressive. I was wondering why he chose that spot as higher vantage points are at his disposal.

I wonder why he's here; I haven't seen him before. Surely there are more lucrative areas in which to search for breakfast. Atop the knotty fence post he sits, me looking at him and him occasionally at me.

Yuri, the stud field mouse who lived in the fence row next to the pond, is no longer with us. He fell prey one night recently as Kitty was making her nightly perimeter patrols. Is he waiting in vain, I wonder if the hawk knows?

As we each sit looking at each other on a chosen piece of wood at a chosen time I don't believe he cares that the grass between us needs mowing and the pipe to the spigot at the corner post needs covering up.

He lost not one minute of sleep caring if the two sapling grape vines get transplanted behind his current perch or not. He doesn't care that I could use one more cup before getting up and getting started.

He has no concern whatsoever if the tractor will crank or a row gets plowed under for taters next month. He cares not one iota if there's enough money in my pocket for seed and fertilizer and a new hoe handle.

His gaze and his presence this morning did serve as a tangible reminder of the words in Matthew: "Look at the birds of the air, for they neither sow nor reap nor gather into barns; yet your heavenly Father feeds them. Are you not of more value than they? Which of you by worrying can add one cubit to his stature?"

As suddenly as the sun shone through the haze, he spread his wings, sailed off his post and into the grass, gathered a small critter and flew aloft with his breakfast.

At the same moment the back door opened, and a bowl of grits and a fresh cup was handed to me.

Thank you, Lord, for another beautiful day....

Empty Chairs

It was blistering hot when our bus rolled into Ft. Benning, Georgia, in July of '82 and there was frost on the ground when I rode out in my brother's ol' International Scout.

Very difficult it is to describe in words the transformation that occurred there, nor is there enough room on this paper or enough ink in the bottle.

Twas one of the most profound and enlightening experiences of my young life.

Every day across our land from the Navy yards of San Diego to Parris Island on the Carolina coast, from Cape May in Jersey to the runways of Lackland AFB in San Antonio, young men and women are being instilled with a sense of pride and a love of country that transcends public opinion. Within these barracks and on these training grounds, they are indwelled with a newfound respect for self and mankind.

In them we have hope. We need them; they need us. Though they are young and strong, fit and bright, the odds are against them.

They are taught that a soldier does not fight because he hates what is in front of him but because he LOVES what is behind him. What is behind them is us.

Tis the same for the local Deputy that puts on a uniform in the morning and patrols our streets, the volunteer firefighter who gets out of a warm bed to fight a fire in the middle of the night and then drudges into his regular job in the morning. To Marine Patrol officers and all first responders – our hats are off to you.

Just like the Infantry they are the boots on the ground, they are the front line of our protection. On nights, weekends, holidays, during (and after) the Super bowl and pouring rain they choose a hard living of sacrifice for their love of humanity and their community.

Not every soldier sees combat, some do. Some will never come home. Not every cop fires a weapon, some do. Some leave home for their daily shift and never return.

Many picnic tables will have an empty spot today.

This is the true meaning of Memorial Day....... the empty chairs.

As the smoke drifts, the ribs sizzle, and the kids splash in the pool, it would be only fitting and proper to take a moment, just a moment and remember a veteran. Also fitting and proper is it to instill this respect in the coming generation. They learn quickest by observation.

Tell the fuzz that you appreciate what they do, buy your paramedic and firefighter a cold drink and say thank you.

We live in America - land of the free, BECAUSE of the brave.

Twas Early September

Under cobalt blue skies flocks of black crows dotted now empty corn fields, it was mid-September and endless rows of waist high cotton stood tall against the afternoon sun. Rugged men in faded overalls sat atop John Deere tractors as rising dust from red clay peanut fields painted everything it touched the color of rusty crimson.

Red Georgia clay to some is measured as the eighth wonder of the world. It can retain the tiniest drop of water in the middle of a hunerd-acre field; it can also retain a two-ton truck in that same field with that same drop of water. Ah, but the produces of its bounty are undeniable.

"And the Lord God formed man from the dust of the ground." It's written, I believe it and I'd like to think He was standing just west of the Flint River when He reached down and got a handful.

As the kids and I rolled onto the farm with ladder stands and ratchets, limb saws, hatchets and high expectations one of my buddies was standing on the porch looking a mite somber.

Word had just been received that we failed to make the short list for the upcoming Fall Exposé in Southern Living. This meant no personal interviews, no four-page glossy photo cabin layout. Our dreams of making the cover were dashed in an instant. *And with all the spiffing up we'd done.........* wood split and neatly stacked, the leak on the roof delicately tarred over while tied off to the chimney with jumper cables.

The slight draft inside had finally been addressed by a series of hanging tapestries acquired from the Good Will collection. And by unanimous decision, we'd gone with two-ply scratchin paper in the outhouse this year. For our cabin to not make the cut was a mental and emotional blow.

Beginning the long-awaited season of whitetail chasing on a negative note is extremely disheartening. A true warrior, however, realizes that it's just a moment in time, a mere obstacle to overcome, he gathers himself mentally and proceeds forth.

The current inhabitants of her surroundings are comprised of bankers and brokers, welders and Boy Scout leaders, entrepreneurs and Sunday school teachers. As the Big Dipper begins to balance herself in the Autumn sky each Fall these diverse characters converge at the block house with a common interest.

We see each other but once a year, sit around a fire, laugh, reminisce and forget about life for a day. And so it was.

Awoke this morning to suddenly realize it is now mid-January and have departed are the boys of winter. Gone already is the smell of smoke and the sound of the axe. Gone for a year is the sight of a strapping young lad skinning a buck and not asking for help.

Brisk afternoons spent with a daughter as we discuss life, boys and bullet trajectories are now no more than memories. Gone is the rustic camaraderie and esprit de corps that define us when the cold winds blow.

Hopes and dreams we must keep tucked in our pockets. I'm hoping with a fresh coat of paint and a checkered tablecloth that we'll have a shot at the Spring cabin exposé.

But for now….. it's just a moment in time.

Sandal Prints

Flat on his back he lay, the ground was hard, but he'd grown quite familiar with that. Had he been knocked down or simply collapsed? He wasn't sure.

Regardless, the man awoke looking skyward and a million pinholes of light scattered across a canvas of black were twinkling back at him.

Often times before this upward view had ushered a sense of peace over him. Now he lay motionless trying to recall the steps of his journey that had led him to this point…………wherever *this* was.

He lay quietly, eyes closed, mind clear and spoke with the One closest to him, the One who created the stars.

He asked for wisdom in order to parry the darts and daggers already in flight toward him. He asked for strength and courage to stand against what was coming.

Others counted on him, their faces fresh in his mind.

Now on his feet he stood looking in all directions. Nothing but emptiness lay between him and the horizons. The man had seen this before, but at a distance while someone else faced their own fears.

Today he stood alone, his horse gone, his pockets empty, and he was out of bullets.

In the past this solitary condition was one he had often sought for and become pleasingly accustomed to.

This day, however, was much different. An intangible dread and a strong sense of unease filled his throat as he stood turning in a circle.

The joys of yesterday were as far away as Orion's belt and tomorrow is never promised. Today and what one does with it is all that ever matters.

A sudden gust of wind blew the hat from his head exposing a pair of tired wrinkled eyes that thought they'd seen it all. The blow came from nowhere. Or had it? Maybe it had been coming all along, and he had just missed the signs.

Now a long deep rumble from a distance sounded its presence behind the wind and darkness followed.

Storms a-comin and this'uns a humdinger. Every fiber from his greying temples down sensed it and he felt empty inside.

Retreat has never been an option for him and being born with no reverse hasn't always been a blessing. Not that either would be of benefit here, but any alternative would be a welcomed consideration. There is nowhere to go, and the fury is coming fast.

The man knew others have stood and faced even greater odds than he. He certainly isn't the first, but he is weary, so weary. Sometimes a stand is not worth the cost, the juice just isn't worth the squeeze. Today it is.

So he stands, though he really doesn't want to. Just to lay back down, close his eyes and think of the night sky and what is beyond would be much more pleasant.

Life seems to have an endless supply of uncertainty and pain. And for that, man needs an endless supply of hope and peace when chaos swirls.

The man had earlier asked for wisdom. He was given a problem to solve. He had asked for strength and courage for it was duly needed. He was granted a danger to overcome.

Now the storm sees a lone soul, standing and casting but a small weak shadow on the ground. The storm doesn't see the sandal prints in the sand next to the man. And therein lies all the difference.

10th of October 2018

Twas the 10th of October, and a monster was beginning to lick the dunes eighteen miles south of the house. It was after dark when we arrived the night before at the deer camp in South Georgia, cats and dogs and spiders alike. They made the ride with mixed emotions, much like myself.

Never run have I, never gave ground, never once backed up even an inch though it would have been beneficial to do so. The decision to leave was spur of the moment and most difficult, and if it was only myself to consider, I may not have done so.

The eyewall was projected to pass within a few miles of our back porch.

In the span of an hour, less time than it takes to give a cat a bath, less time than it takes a University of Florida lineman to find his butt with both hands four vehicles were loaded and north bound.

Some things were obviously necessary, insurance policies, bullets, birth certificates, leftover cornbread, passports, King James Version and a few more bullets.

It was the next fifty-five minutes that a soul needs to ponder a bit and there was no time to ponder. *There were still dishes in the sink.*

Knowing the Big Wind Cometh and the hounds were at the door causes the body to stir a bit inside. Though a peace I really can't explain was present, the process became fast and furious. Cash to get, medicine, groceries and ice chests, and all in an hour's time.

There was so much to leave behind, so many fly rods and hand-tied Bea Bea Bugs that may never again ripple the water. The younguns were instructed in like manner. Take only what is essential.

The next half hour was, to the casual observer, a case study in psychology 101.

Mariah, my daughter of eighteen years, gathered a hundred handwritten journals, stuffed them in a bag and left all her clothes. Cradled her guitar, a fiddle and left behind a stuffed hope chest of heirloom items. Her bed was neatly made.

Beau, a year his sister's junior, started taking deer heads off the wall and left family portraits behind. He scanned the fridge for anything transportable then added extra food in his fish tank, tapped his finger on the glass and bid his Tetras farewell. His bed wasn't made.

Jennifer coaxed two dogs and four cats into her car, an overnight bag with no curling iron and a half-charged Kindle.

In my truck was an ax, generator, some tools and a coupla gas of cans. A bag of chew on the dash and a quart of oil in the floorboard.

Comes into consideration at times like this all the junk we hold dear to us, or think is dear to us. We drag this stuff around like Linus's blanket and try to protect it at all costs. In actuality, we are merely passing through a series of days and nights on this earth waiting on the trumpet to sound.

We should never allow anything tangible to make or break us mentally or emotionally.

It was a grand reminder for me. That hour of decision. Almost fifty-eight years of accumulation to fit in a truck bed in a few moment's time.

With vehicles sparsely loaded we gathered in the flowerbed by the front porch, laid hands on the house and prayed for its protection. We should have done it for the pole barn and shed also.

Within the time span of a round of golf, within the time span of a little league game this monster laid waste to over a billion dollars of timber and incalculable amounts of enjoyable shade. It destroyed thousands of dreams and changed the course of countless lives in less time than it took Broward county to count the votes.

Reduced to less than kindling and scrap metal, our pile of dreams and memories grew each day across the street - **as did our hopes for a better tomorrow.**

As I am mercifully granted an opportunity to begin again with old bones and new eyes, our new course will be much different. A needed purge was amply provided and a clearer understanding adhered to.

To have more, we should simply desire less.

A Daughter's Request

Came to me rather humbly she did. "Daddy can we do something different this year?" It was late October, and I was in the swing consumed in my own thoughts. Her words caught me off guard. We, like everyone else, were attempting to reestablish some sort of routine in the aftermath of a cat-5 hurricane. Trying to get back in the groove – and wondering if the groove even existed. At that point any sense of normalcy would have been comforting. …. What creatures of habit we have become, I remember thinking.

She stood on the porch and made her request, this daughter of mine. "Let's go away somewhere for Christmas, it doesn't have to be far, let's just go."

At one matriarch's home or another we'd always gathered. Grand- or great-grandmothers' homes were the point of congregation on Christmas morning. Now, a huge void looms before us, all our matriarchs have recently crossed over Jordan, and this daughter of mine was desperately trying to prepare and adapt.

Christmas morning traditions in our family are few — but well-grounded and adhered to. Fried chicken for breakfast was the hard and fast rule, grits, gravy, biscuits and OJ. Plenty of fried chicken, and not store-bought. After the bones were piled up and the belching had begun, we'd gather by the fireplace and read, usually Luke chapter 2.

Sometimes Mama'd find a heartfelt story or poetic card, once she found a letter sent from an Uncle overseas during the war in the '40s. She made certain our perspective of Christmas was proper before tearing paper on the gifts. This was our routine, then fresh oysters for a late lunch.

Our Christmas tree was a live one dug up in the woods or sometimes nursery bought. Then around New Year's, we'd replant it in the front yard. A visual reminder of seasons past in staggering height, all destroyed on October 10th.

How would it feel I wondered, if we departed our standing routines and did not share a plate or a cup of nog with my siblings and kin on Christmas morning? Not even having a tree? Benedict Arnold came to mind.

We left everyone we knew to spend a holiday with folks we'd never seen. The deer camp was a stopping point on our way to a rocking chair on a lazy street in the Georgia foothills. Before leaving the cabin for our intended destination, Beau dug up a tree in the woods and brought it in for our return. A nice touch I thought.

After a few nights in a rented bed with an indoor shower and two days of smiling strangers at a festival of lights, bakeries and coffee on an oddly familiar street in small town Americana, our new jaunt had run its course.

Christmas Eve found us again traveling south and trying to wrap our heads around this newfound custom.

Back at the cabin we awoke snuggled under blankets with no alarm clock and no agenda. The fireplace in the crusty room roared and the coffee perked. There was silence outside on this frosty Christmas morning, utter silence in these lonely woods. There was grits, there was gravy and the biscuits were rising nicely. We had no chicken. We had forgotten the chicken. Six pounds of fudge and two pies on the table, but we had no fried chicken.

Days earlier we'd visited a small church in a quaint town in the hills. The message, however, in this small church was huge, and we took it to heart. A Christmas full of happiness, regardless of where it's celebrated, will be full of peace and harbor no regrets. It will be absent of pretention and full of humility.

The pastor spoke nothing of gifts or nog or even chicken.

The Spot

The bucket on which he sat was hard and too low for comfort. Perfectly good chairs were in reach and a few had cushions. He didn't know why he chose the bucket. Its position offered no shade; he chuckled a bit and mused inwardly that shade in the near future would certainly come at a premium.

Maybe because it was where he used to sit at this hour. Strategically located it was, in order to absorb the majesty of each sunrise as the rays filtered thru the pines to the east. Sometimes on the cold, dreary mornings a mist would rise from the pond and those early rays would slowly sway a bit, sorta side-to-side. Kinda like the girls being swooned from the saxophone of Dirty Lenny and the Speak Easy Band.

Maybe it was because on the rainy mornings, it was just far enough from the barn's eve to keep his shirt sleeve dry. And on those still, muggy mornings when sweat drops as big as marbles ran down your back, a floor fan provided enough breeze to tilt your cap.

He liked this spot, and it liked him. Until recently a small, rickety table just big enough for a coffee cup and a whet rock leaned next to his chair. This took care of the 'idle hands' his mama warned him about.

As the coffee perked each morning, he would anxiously await what would be seen from where the bucket now sat. Each day was different now, *post-hurricane*. And yet every day was the same depending on the viewpoint of the soul. Some days from this spot one could watch a woodpecker bang his head against an oak in a furious attempt at breakfast. Early hours in late fall were serenaded by the callings of Bob White and his Whipowill friends. And in spring when the Honey-suckle blooms, butterflies and bees are buzzing and flittering all about, living in perfect harmony. All one had to do was sit still and watch from this spot.

From here you could see the grape vines bud out and young oaks stretching to the blue while spreading wide their arms. He had secretly hoped one day the kids and maybe grandkids might sit under their cool shade and ponder their life path. From this location one could hear the crow of a rooster and the moo of a cow in duet fashion.

From this spot one could learn to listen, really listen. A soul could learn to see instead of just look. What he sees now is nothing familiar of what once was.

Solomon left us with some interesting words. "A man's heart plans his course, but the Lord determines his steps." I wonder what event led Solomon to this insight, did it come at sunrise as his plans for the day suddenly went amiss? Had he envisioned a very clear and decisive path for his family, and in an instant the path disappeared?

In the aftermath, from this spot, I am now afforded a brand spanking new view of the same sun complete with old dreams. Who knows, it may be even better in time.

Perhaps we are intended to find a new spot. Maybe we are supposed to slow down, read and listen more and talk and write less. Perhaps it is time to slide a charcoal pencil across textured paper, shade it just right and draw something perty or even stroke some oil paint on canvas. Spend more time behind a camera lens maybe and less time in front of a computer screen. Maybe, just maybe it is time to mend a needed fence and forgive a transgression.

Perhaps it is time to find a quiet spot and read Psalms 46:10.

Finally

Finally… things are as they should be. Arose, donned my robe and Jennifer met me in the kitchen with coffee and bacon.

Walked out to the porch, the air was crisp. Henrietta was restless on her perch, a crescent moon rose high overhead and the belt of Orion was sinking slowly on the western horizon.

The elements of natured appeared to be in perfect harmony this morning. *And*…………..

There was **frost** on my breath. It was as welcomed as one would welcome the return of a prodigal child. Standing there and taking it all in, I walked to the corner of the porch and reached around to turn on the shower, and …..

…. *nothing*. The showerhead was frozen. I actually smiled; it was my first sign that quite possibly things are finally as they should be for late November.

Two Bears

The wrestling of two bears is a continuous event in my mirror most mornings. On a regular basis they arrive and square off as I attempt to slide razor across a stubby cheek. One bear answers to *ignorance,* and the other I call *apathy.*

Well aware am I that ignorance is merely a personal choice and adopting an attitude of apathy is but a single step from the undertaker.

I did make attempts to fight the bear of ignorance by learning the goings on of my immediate surroundings. I would occasionally watch the local news and expand from there to state and national platforms. I tried to listen and learn, I really did.

But as soon as the tube came on, twenty-eight minutes of turmoil, violence, and disrespect are pumped into my living room. All of this chaos followed by a ninety-second inspirational puff piece about a rescued kitten at the end. And this perty much sums up a typical newscast. A wasted half-hour of my life.

The baffling part to me is... for all those who continually express their distrust and discontent for national media and the NFL .... they sit each day with bated breath and never miss a single minute of broadcasts and never fail to repost it on social media, thus keeping the chaos and carnage alive. *Baffling.*

Time has become very, very precious to me. There is no room for this in my day, and I refuse to subject myself to it. Call me ignorant if you will. I've been called worse. It is peaceful on my porch, and there are options. I – just like you – are granted a certain number of breaths on this earth. Refuse do I to waste any of mine on rhetoric such as this when natural, pleasant options are readily available.

Apathy, I also realize is just as destructive. And, the old adage remains true, "If you don't stand for something, you'll fall for anything." I believe a soul needs a purpose and something to believe in. A person with no purpose or conviction each day tends to be little more than a shell with the nut long dried up. If there were nothing to struggle for, nothing would be achieved. And personally, I feel that no one is worth their salt unless they have at some point won OR lost a battle on principle.

I may be wrong ... but I still subscribe to the theory that hard work and clean-living builds character. And good character will triumph at the end of the road whether there is a trophy at the end or not.

My responsibility is not to ensure that my younguns or yours grow up in the same environment as we did; that world vanished with Ronald Reagan and Blue Suede Shoes. My job is to prepare them to navigate on their own the storm of an ever-changing culture.

Hmmm, maybe I could teach them to whip the bear of apathy by 'being the storm.' Anything is possible, for they have seen me successfully beat the pants off anorexia. And many have watched gravity beat the pants off me.

The laws of nature still hold true today and more importantly, the laws of an unchanging God. Undeniably they have stood the test of time and provide man with the only true source of inner peace.

This is my daily battle. I cannot stop the chaos or statues from coming down or the polar ice caps from melting. But I can choose today and tomorrow what I read and what I listen to.

Daydreaming

A dream I have harbored for years on end has been the ability to spend an entire hunting season at the ol' camp on Cook Farm.

Back in the '90s, my first foray into this crusty cabin was greeted by an aging, towering feller named Stamps. He was a long-time friend of Charles Cook, the property owner and a character in his own right. Mr. Stamps stood 6'6" and drove a gold Cadillac Coupe Deville with white leather interior. This was his huntin buggy. Stamps was an ex-golf pro that lived in a citrus grove in central Florida. He spent his winters in the old Georgia cabin.

Each April he made his way north to Augusta to stand amongst the rest to watch the big boys tee-off and chase the coveted green jacket at the Master's tournament. But when October rolled around, he would pull up to the old huntin cabin with a single suitcase, a box of bullets and a loaf of bread prepared to settle in once again for the winter.

I often wondered what it would be like to spend three months a year out of the rat race, three consecutive, solitary months in a rustic cabin with only an outhouse and a fireplace. To have nine hundred acres of a natural hardwood playground at your fingertips. *Aahhh.... to live like Stamps.*

On many a frosty morning as the rest of us hustled and scrambled to get to our deer stands, Stamps never rolled over, never got up. Other days, he'd be stirring around having cereal and toast, then stroll out to the woods at first light. On the coldest of days, he'd simply put another log on the fire and crawl back under his blanket. Age and wisdom I guess, had taught him when to stay and when to go.

Past years found me with a copiously loaded truck on Friday mornings driving to work. And when the whistle finally blew in the afternoon we screamed north to the timber. For two days a week we'd stalk the woods and ponds with a vengeance and seldom slept for fear of missing even the slightest of opportunities.

We'd then drive a hunerd and fifty miles back home just in time to shower, choke down a biscuit and repeat our dreaded work week. Before Thanksgiving arrived, the lot of us resembled a sack of earthworms with the guts slung out. Mr. Stamps, then pushing eighty, was just hitting his stride.

Time and circumstance eventually provided me with an opportunity to live the dream for a season.

The afforded time came in the form of an exit from a demanding career of the past twenty years and fourteen years of self-employment prior to that. The opportunity arrived in a well-planned reduction of responsibility for a six-month period. *Aahhh...... to live like Stamps*, even for a brief period.

Finally, for me was the ability to warm my feet by the fire with no rush to get home. No pressing engagements or obligations to prevent a Monday morning rendezvous with a monster whitetail. And after everyone else had departed, I held the personal option of sleeping-in, if so desired. It had been a long time coming. Finally, the opportunity to sit in chilly silence and gaze upon the night sky with only the flicker of flame as a companion.

Then came Michael. He arrived in the form of a wind event on a Cat-5 magnitude. A destroyer of dreams was he, and on an unprecedented scale. Our wonderland in the woods was destroyed in the equivalent of a single workday of a twenty-year career. The roof left the cabin and so did the outhouse with a fresh stock of two-ply striking paper. Still, we came and stayed and enjoyed each other's company. This place beckons to me.

The boys of winter were there, all reeling fresh in the aftermath, trying to enjoy what was left of our once hardwood wonderland.

As *Robert Burns* once wrote, "The best laid plans of mice and men often go awry."

For each of us to live the life, live our dream, we must be able to willingly adjust and adapt to changing conditions. "To make the best of a bad situation," as *Mike Whitfield* would say.

"All men dream, but not equally. Those who dream by night in the dusty recesses of their minds, wake in the day to find that it was vanity: but the dreamers of the day are dangerous men, for they may act on their dreams with open eyes, to make them possible."   *T.E. Lawrence*

My dream was finally at hand, but it was like trying to firmly grasp and hold a handful of water.

Eyes Wide Open

It was the break of a twig that jolted my eyes wide open. Now they were darting to and fro searching, searching. How long were they shut, I wondered? It was pitch dark when I arrived and began my ascent, feeling my way up the cold steel rungs as I climbed.

The light was dim now, just beginning to filter through the trees as it danced with the morning fog. Another snapped twig and two very cautious steps behind me..... then silence. Heart thumping now and mad at myself for not eating another biscuit because the rumble in my stomach could be heard in the next county. I dared not blink nor twitch a muscle.

My ears were ice cubes and my toes were tingling despite two pair of socks. I noticed the frost from my breath was wafting straight up, that was good. It's bewildering how the entire body can reach full alert and aware of every sensory nerve in .89 seconds from a sound, relaxed state.

Another step, it's closer now. Suddenly, my peripheral vision detected movement on the left side of the tree – dark heavy beams of horn adorned his head and the icy breath from his nose was rising skyward as well.

Instinctively reaching for my bow, I noticed frost on the shaft and the 3-blade Muzzy that crowned its tip. I prayed it wouldn't make a squeak as it was lifted from its holder.

He stood there motionless looking away as if something had his attention. This was a gift.

It never happens like this. Two more steps forward produced a Patriarch of behemoth proportions rippled with muscle at a mere eleven yards. Now the bow was coming to full draw, thumb anchored firmly on cheek, nose on the string and sights lined up….. then ………

I sat straight up, bent at a 90-degree angle wide-eyed again and gasping desperately for breath that was not there.

It was at this moment that Babu, our 'other' cat, had decided to stand on the off button of my CPAP machine beside the bed.......................
some dreams never die.

Growin Up 'n Catchin On

"Good luck, Daddy, hope you get one, I love you."

He stood quietly gathering his gear beside the truck. I wanted him to hurry because the mercury read 33 degrees and the stiff draft from the open door was touching me on the nose. All of his necessities were now accounted for and off he trod into the darkness.

I knew he had a long walk, but it was one of his choosing. There was no moon tonight and the night sky was clear and brilliant. Thousands upon thousands of twinkling pin holes on an endless, mesmerizing black canvas with so many stories to tell. I wondered if he'd pause in the middle of the peanut field to admire it as I'd done many times before.

Taught was he to use no light in the open and very little on the trails when pursuing a trophy, and I saw no flicker as the cold, crisp darkness engulfed him, and I smiled.

It was still long before the first hint of light would begin to creep through the swamp bottom for which he headed, and the ground underneath would crunch with every step. The cold metal rungs on the ladder were going to moan and sound their disapproval when he climbed, and I hoped he'd remember these things.

I now sat on a log looking over a creek bed awaiting the sun and thinking of these things, of the disciplines necessary to be successful in any life endeavor. Finding the fortitude to brave the elements and face each day regardless of the circumstances. To learn to rely on no one else and use the talents you've been given and use them well. To look forward to each sunrise with – if nothing else – an optimistic attitude.

Deer hunting for our family is an opportunity to enhance and build on these disciplines; they are solitary by design. Whether the freezer gets filled and we eat meat in the spring solely depends on you and well…….. sometimes luck.

An hour before he'd awoke to only a dim resemblance of the roaring fire that blazed when he pulled the heavy blanket over his head hours earlier. In a quickness it roared again, and the small, crusty room was again tolerable for a moment. He'd scarfed down a stack of waffles and a coupla eggs like they were the last ones on earth. With a cup of coffee under his belt he went out to warm the truck and bring in more lighter'd for the fire. A tangerine tucked in his pocket for later on and an extra bullet, just in case.

His routine was becoming impressive, and he is beginning to catch on. I pondered these things and was pleased.

About mid-morning he texted and said he was headed to the extraction point. I met him at the wood line, and he told me of his morning's experience and how it unfolded. He described in detail a gut feeling and why he had decided to act contrary to it. We talked of this lesson learned as we drove across the field, him empty handed.

Through the woods we drove in silence and as we neared the camp, I finally asked him if he'd mind helping me skin, clean and quarter mine.

"You didn't need any help pulling the trigger, you shouldn't need any help now. I'm taking a nap."

I do believe he's catching on........

Take Nothing for Granted

I was jolted from my sleep by a screaming, hysterical wife. Not the kind of scream when you almost step on a snake, the kind you turn loose when a hungry bobcat has both jaws clamped on your butt and won't let go. She was running to and fro through the house, wailing and flinging her arms trying to shake this unseen cat. I knew this day had already gone terribly wrong and dawn had just broken.

A good friend was standing in the yard with his hands in his pockets and looking down at the ground. Being a visually oriented person – I knew this was not a good sign. He'd come to deliver the news.

I stood still, trying to move but couldn't. Maybe because of the lack of coffee injection and my limbs weren't yet functioning properly, maybe because her words were starting to sink in. "The kids have been in a wreck, and it's bad!"

Out the door we ran, my friend standing there, solemn. It was drizzling rain I remember, and I hadn't bothered to hook the other side of my overalls or put my boots on.

Mind going in a thousand directions at once, we didn't speak a word to each other. For five or six miles at a hundred miles an hour, silent prayers flooded heaven.

An ambulance, coupla firetrucks, three State Troopers and flashing lights were everywhere when we rounded the curve at the ol' dump. I was numb. I parked behind the three Troopers (that was a first). They were casually talking to each other, looked in my direction, then down at the ground. Indescribable is one's feelings at this moment. Already numb, now an empty sickening feeling that til now was unknown to me.

Crossing the road toward the ambulance another good friend saw me and lifted his hand.

I interpreted it as a gesture to stop where I was. Man, the mind swirl and the gut wrench were almost too much. Then I saw the wreckage. It got worse, and I just stood there frozen in the road.

I remember seeing many familiar faces, many childhood friends – now first responders. None were smiling.

My kids had gotten up early and gone to the church to finish their custodial tasks. They were returning home when, in an instant, our lives took a turn.

Everything in my life changed that day. My perception of today, of tomorrow, of right now will hopefully never again be taken for granted. What used to be important, no longer is. What used to worry me, no longer does. What before seemed to bring me little happiness, now overwhelms me.

That was Christmas Eve of 2017. My children, only by the grace of God, are alive and well today.

Never again will Christmas be about presents under the tree, how many or how few. Never again will it be associated with a huge spread on the table or even saddened if it's not. Never again will it be associated with festivities or mistletoe or any material thing. We will remain humble and grateful and laugh every day as much as humanly possible.

Jennifer and I received the second-best Christmas present one could imagine that day. The lives of our children. And for however long they are granted to us will be cherished. The very best gift is the undying love of Christ that made the second gift possible.

Heroes Walk Among Us

The distinctive sound of a radio pierces the still darkness, situation and location are the only words squawking in his ears as both eyes slam wide open.

Covers are thrown back and feet touch floor in a hurry. A pair of rubber bibs hangs on a hook nearby and tall, well-worn boots stand ready by the door. With these donned, he's down the steps with sleep in his eyes and an empty spot in his belly where a biscuit should be. There's no time for coffee or to kiss his own kids goodbye.

Whatever his plans for this day will have to wait, a long-awaited opportunity to visit his honey hole in Trout's Kitchen is now postponed. Perhaps he was planning to wrap his hands around a garden plow or maybe even his wife.

Possibly he was looking forward to sleeping past first light and enjoying his coffee on the porch. Quite often these bibs and boots are put on before his regular workday begins.

Sometimes it is freezing cold and pouring rain in the wee hours when the call comes. At others it is in the middle of a birthday celebration or during the ninth inning of the seventh game. Occasionally he's merely sitting in a chair with his eyes closed after pulling an arduous ten-hour shift. Regardless, the call is answered, and the boots are worn.

When he arrives, sometimes he'll take charge and give commands, other times he'll drag a heavy hose as far as it'll reach or pry open a door with special tools. Teamwork is the key; each does as needed at the time, for every call is unlike the last and different from the next.

What now seems a lifetime ago I walked in a daze across the highway amongst flashing lights of every color, past State Troopers, paramedics, a pastor, and the guys in rubber boots as they strode to and fro all busy in various roles.

Some had driven the big trucks with flashing lights and sirens, some stood and directed traffic, others applied metal-bending, life-saving devices, others mended wounds and stopped the bleeding while guiding a disoriented lad to safety. One extended his arm through a broken window and simply held the hand of a little girl as utter chaos swirled around them.

On this day and every day to come I will be forever grateful to them.

They do not receive a paycheck for their services; they do not shirk the responsibilities handed them, and they do not kneel for the National Anthem. These talented, dedicated, community loving volunteers seldom receive recognition for their deeds and sacrifices, nor do they expect to.

These heroes wear no numbered jersey, no distinguished crown and yet they walk among us every day.

And only when the last shard of glass is cleaned up, only when the last flicker of flame is extinguished, and the last light is turned off will the boots and bibs stand ready again by the door.

Mariah's Buck

"Daddy, if it's okay I'm going to drive up after we get through at the church Thursday night and stay at the camp with y'all. This way I can get in two morning and two afternoon hunts with you." Talk about music to a daddy's ears; I hear a lot of music in my house, but none as sweet as this.

At the time, my oldest was seventeen, fiercely independent, worked a 40+ hour work week and showed no permanent sign of scarring where the apron strings were severed long, long ago. It's a hunerd and thirty-five miles from our front door to the small red reflector marking the obscure trail leading into the South Georgia camp. Because the road less traveled has always appealed to me, there are only two red lights on this route tween our house and there. Most of it is back country roads with rusty mailboxes and grain silos providing landmarks.

She'd done it once before alone in the daylight, but darkness was the prevailing feature on this trip. GPS is maybe fifty percent effective in this neck of the woods, sunlight is usually a day late and the folks back here are just learning of the Kennedy assassination.

She made, with much prayer, the trip alone just fine.

Upon her arrival her brother had one already skinned and in the box. The pressure of sibling rivalry inched upward before she got to her bunk. Their give-and-take in this arena is fun to watch………. sometimes.

Two pair of socks and a fireplace were the only provisions of warmth at her disposal. Her brother split the wood, and they laid a fire. Daddy's job was simply to provide breakfast, encouragement, ammunition, direction to the stand and maybe a few words of advice.

For a day and a half, they traversed the woods to and fro with the wildest of dreams no doubt of what could be across the next creek bottom. Each day they saw deer, each day they both watched bucks. But as is more often case, you walk back to the camp empty handed, build a fire and take a nap.

On her last afternoon some good friends invited us over for an evening hunt and a change of scenery. She was handling the ninth inning pressure well up to this point. As we were climbing into the stand a shot rang nearby meaning someone else had a deer or hog destined for the skinning pole. Ten minutes later her brother texted and reported that he had two deer down for the afternoon and wanting permission to shoot a third.

Sibling rivalry had just touched the bottom rung of the upper echelon, and I could feel it four feet away. It was here an opportunity for 'life lessons to come' presented itself. We talked of perseverance, of simply finding satisfaction with knowing you did your very best. I told her that seldom do events ever unfold as we imagine, and that pre-meditating can be a dangerous and disappointing term, *especially if it's slung around in a court room.* I also mentioned that it only takes a few seconds or less to change your entire life and that being prepared will always tilt the odds in your favor.

"Daddy there's a deer on the wood line, and it's a good buck, a ten point I think." My ol' binoculars weren't much good, but I could tell he was a hoss. Well, baby girl, use your best judgement and you don't have long. "I'm gonna shoot when he clears those bushes."

Her composure appeared much superior to mine at this juncture. I remember the click as she flipped off the safety and knew it was coming. She squeezed the trigger and the ol' beast dropped like a prom dress.

After hugs and high fives, we stood and talked of his role as an obvious patriarch and how he had contributed to his herd and how we were grateful for him now contributing to us.

For some it's a homerun or a touchdown, for others it's standing and reciting a line in a play. For a few it's simply watching your children begin to make sound fundamental decisions.

For my Mama it was anything above a 'C' on a report card and coming home without blood loss. Regardless, days like this are few and far between and must be truly savored.

We had a sack full of younguns in camp over Thanksgiving, and the little ones had scribbled on the camp wall, "Girls kill big bucks." Today those words rang true.

The Circle of Rabbits

Learned last night that yet another friend left the world unexpectedly and much too soon. That's two in the last ten days and this sets the mind adrift. Drives to the surface it does one of my truest fears. Is my family ready when the buzzards are circling as my name is called?

Will they fall apart and be unable to function or will they stand? Have they been pointed in the right direction? Has there been enough porch-time discussion on the evils of loose women and smooth whisky?

Did it sink in? Only time and faith will tell. Has the quest for wisdom and knowledge been properly instilled, and the difference between the two made clear? Can the boy immediately assume the role needed, plumb a busted pipe at 2 a.m. in the freezing rain? Provide and protect with a smile when the wolves are at the door? Can the girl change a tire in the dark alone? Can she hit a moving target at fifty yards? Can she make something from nothing, provide needed nourishment from an empty pantry?

I ponder these things in the stillness of my mind.

More importantly, will they rest their head knowing they were loved and adored, and not only by their parents? So much emphasis and energy are exerted on preparing children for success and prosperity. They are encouraged and taught to grasp ahold of this world with both hands and a pair of pliers. Most of them receive precious little instruction on exiting it and the personal effects associated with it.

When my oldest, Mariah Rain was a wee lass of five we raised rabbits and a litter was had by one of the does. She loved those little furry balls and would sneak one into her bed at night to cuddle. Jennifer would have to return it to the pen with a flashlight after she nodded off to sleep.

I walked into the living room after work one afternoon to ankle-deep crocodile tears. She wailed and shook and sobbed and hyperventilated because one of her fuzzy little balls had died. I took her outside with me, buried the tiny rabbit and walked her over to the pen. I showed her the mama with six other nursing babies and told her the mama, even though she was sad, still had responsibilities to the others.

She learned it was perfectly natural to grieve and be saddened, but one still had to carry on. Coming home from the feed store a few days later I found her eating a bowl of cereal on the porch but was a little damp around the eyes. I asked what was wrong. "Another baby rabbit died, the spotted one." OK, baby girl, I'll change clothes and we'll go bury it. "Daddy, I already did, and the Mama is ok." ……….. and thus, to her, the circle of life was grasped.

Most men I associate with will stand defiantly on a hilltop for the sake of family and take on a thunderstorm with a pitchfork in each hand.

We will anguish in silence, and we will bleed to the last drop for our loved ones. We will scrape and plan and make numerous sacrifices to give them an edge. We will fervently justify our actions and motives in terms of bettering their health, education and profession, all in a summary term we call success.

I carry a much different definition of success and have done my best to pass this on to them.

And to paraphrase *Bessie Stanley's* 1904 poem defining success: a successful person at the end of his days will have held the admiration of his peers and small children. They will have left their space better than they found it. They will have been certain of their destination and been well prepared to die.

We Blendeth Not

The feller on the phone said, "I have it in my hand. It'll go out in the mail today." Whew – Thank You!

As we were driving through the winding pines and hardwoods leading into the Lodge, we met a limo coming out. It was so long the only place he could possibly turn around was the airport. Already having mixed emotions about this not being my kinda place, I kept quiet.

Before we got to the front door, I reminded the kids to secure all firearms, ammo and anything that might be considered an explosive device – this ain't Motel 6. And sure enough, a half dozen valets and bellhops were busy unpacking and stacking Louis Vuitton luggage from the cookie cutter snow bunnies emerging from a line of Benzes and land-yachts. And then there was us...

I popped the trunk on my '08 Crown Vic police interceptor cruising vessel and like a well-oiled machine duffle bags, hardware and other survival necessities were unloaded neatly and in an instant. A valet approached and asked if he could be of assistance, and since he didn't have a wheelbarrow on hand – he couldn't.

I handed Jennifer my wallet to go check in while I parked the car. It was the last time I saw it.

Approximately four hundred yards from the front door, bordering the next county I found an empty space. Oh well, I could use the exercise anyway.

Inside the lobby was nice, not opulent but nice. A twenty-foot perfectly decorated Christmas tree took center stage under the vaulted ceiling. Warm cider and hot chocolate were available by the front door. A quartet donned in Charles Dickens era garb caroled their hearts out as we checked in. Leggings tucked into calf-high boots with fuzzy stuff on top was in abundance, they all looked the same. And then there was us...

"Daddy, we don't exactly blend in." Maybe it was the brogans and duffle bags, maybe it was the overalls with a bleached peace sign on the back pocket. Maybe it was their air of confidence and self-reliance in standing alone that seemed unnatural to others. *Or possibly* it was the venison backstrap that was beginning to thaw out in the overnight bag.

"Children of mine," I said, "you were born to stand out – not blend in. Now git to the room before the meat thaws."

At supper time, after finding that the hotplate had shorted out during the storm and it was a four-hundred-yard trek to the car there was little choice. We found ourselves in the Lodge's dining room strewn with dim twinkling lights, soft music and a festive ambiance. We were, for some reason, seated front and center next to the buffet. This was a first. Farmers Market in Thomasville is good – better'n good actually – but these folks had out done themselves on this night.

Prime rib, oysters on the half-shell, crab legs, seasoned shrimp, smoked ham, chicken fixed a coupla ways, and I can't remember past that. The waddle back to the room was laborious.

Two days later I walked past an elderly gentleman sitting on a bench. "Hey, you look like a banjo picker or something." I stopped in my tracks wondering why he picked me out of a crowd and turned to my son. "Daddy, you remember, we don't blend." I walked over to the feller and replied that though I highly admire banjo pickers, guitar and cotton pickers, I was none of the above. In fact, the only thing I'd ever picked was a tomato and some watermelons once that didn't belong to me. A lengthy, pleasant discussion ensued and at departure I reached in my pocket and gave him my last piece of pecan fudge. I should have noticed it then............

I've often wondered why folks who simply look different are treated diversely and am I guilty of the same? Tried have I to teach my younguns contrary to this behavior, to open and hold a door for all women, young n perty or old n not, black, white or blue – be courteous and helpful to everyone.

A day and a half later and two hundred miles down the road the realization came. My wallet was missing. Not that this was going to cause an adverse effect on Wall Street, I just wanted it back. It's true and very seldom that Franklins or Jacksons or even Washingtons rub against each other in my wallet. But there is information I occasionally need. Sometimes I have to hand my I.D. through the window so an officer can finish his paperwork, I'm helpful that way. And I really didn't want the hassle of reapplying for another carry-conceal card.

We called the Lodge with little optimism of a positive outcome. Knowing full well that most folks in places like that do not give a second thought to folks like us. Besides it'd been two days and many patrons in fuzzy boots later.

After yet another day and a few more calls, the feller on the phone finally said, "I have it in my hand. It'll go out in the mail today, Merry Christmas."

How about that – even for folks who blendeth not, good things sometimes happen.

Pass the Grits

While spending a quiet evening reminiscing with an ol' friend and eating fresh backstrap on the Dead Lakes recently, I remembered this ol' story:

It was in the late 70's the first time I saw this phrase written on a T-shirt of a local band. 'Americans by birth – Southern by the grace of God'. I remember scribbling it on my hardhat when working on a construction crew in Texas and was proud of it then, still am.

The implication is that those of us raised below the Mason-Dixon line are considered 'the chosen.' Ponder this: when we speak of north, east or west these terms are usually directional in nature.

Yet when one mentions the South you can immediately smell the sweet aroma of a honeysuckle bloom, literally taste Tupelo honey drippin offa hot biscuit and hear 'yas'm' and 'y'all' before the mind knows better.

We belong to a storied land of legend, of passion and patriotism. It's been written about and sung about; it's been fought for and died for. Our cherished heritage is one derived of frog legs and fried okra, of steamboats and sassafras, of squirrel hunting and sweet tea. And the Bible Belt cuts a deep and wide swath through this precious, mossy laden expanse we call home. We enjoy the kindest neighbors, the best music, the warmest hearts and the coolest shades. We are blessed with the constant sounds of crickets and swaying porch swings. We relish in 'doin nothin' on a Saturday, and sometimes it takes us all day to get around to it.

A bit of history reading will often try and tout us Southerners as 'free thinkers', maybe even to the extent as to be considered non-conformists. True enough often times it seems our way of thinking rarely coincides with mainstream media. And the only common trait we share with the rest of the country is the English language...... and it took us awhile to perfect that.

Sixteen years ago, my wife n I sat on the grass under the stars and watched the laser light show in Stone Mountain, Ga. It was the most patriotic and inspiring tribute to true Southern Americana I've ever witnessed.

I've said all that to say this: with much freedom comes much responsibility, an area in which I've just realized my own dismal failures. Our way of life and the things we hold dear are but one generation away from being forgotten. Herein lies our personal responsibilities, we must assure that our kids are more familiar with Jefferson Davis, Stephen Foster, Robert E. Lee, Margaret Mitchell, Mark Twain and William Faulkner than they are with any Hollywood celebrity.

They must learn to slow their roll, be gracious and considerate while standing firm and casting a long shadow upon this colorful heritage that has been entrusted to them.

While the rest of the world speeds on, it does hold true that our speech and lifestyles are as slow as a herd of turtles. Yet we usually get to where we're going on time. And though our way of thinking is not perfect by any stretch, we do tend to think for ourselves and seldom follow the crowd.

We fully understand and often tolerate those from afar with a natural desire to enter into our delightful land of mint julep and lazy afternoon naps....... To you we have but one request — change nothing while you're here, and please pass the grits.

Peace y'all

ACKNOWLEDGEMENTS

Undoubtably I would be remiss without giving due credit to those who, though unbeknownst to them, have made this fledgling endeavor possible.

To Mrs. Betty Bidwell and Mrs. Carol Kelley, two of my high school teachers who long ago piqued an interest in a wandering mind to the written word and to the presentation of it.

To my Sunday school class: Leanna, Mike & Lana, Jamey & Jennifer, Megan, Shane, Hal & Melanie, George, Charles & Dawn, Miranda, Bill, Denny & Tracy, to whom each Sunday leaves a positive and indelible impression that helps carry me through the week.

And to my darling wife Jennifer who urged me to write, made it possible so I could and handled all the details.

Made in the USA
Columbia, SC
18 July 2019